A Guide to Long-Term Care Administration

By
Timothy M. Farabaugh

PublishAmerica
Baltimore

First printing

ISBN: 1-4241-4010-2
PUBLISHED BY PUBLISHAMERICA, LLLP
www.publishamerica.com
Baltimore

Printed in the United States of America

Dedication

I would like to thank my wife for her continued support of my ministry to the elderly and to dedicate this book to all those with whom I have worked through the years. Co-workers, supervisors and those whom I have supervised have all contributed in some way to the thoughts and comments found here.

Introduction

Long-term care is a term that refers to care given to residents in nursing facilities, assisted living facilities or continuing care retirement communities. Those who choose to work in this field should be acquainted with the unique needs of the people they serve.

This book will offer a look at the physical, emotional and spiritual needs of the elderly residents who comprise the majority of long-term care residents. Following that glimpse of the typical older adult, the book will continue to focus on the overall administration of a long-term care facility including highlighting the regulations that govern this industry. Those who are preparing to take a state and federal examination to be a licensed administrator will find this book to be a valuable tool. Administrators already working in the field will benefit from the comprehensive look at both the assisted living industry and how it compares to the typical nursing facility in both regulation and function.

Table of Contents

Part One

The information in the first three chapters of this book explains the physical, emotional and spiritual needs of the elderly. Some of this information was also used in my first book entitled, *Ministry to and with the Elderly*. It serves as a beginning point to understanding who the elderly are and what particular needs they have that long-term care administrators can try to meet through nursing, activities, dining and social services.

Chapter One

Understanding the Resident

In most states, there is an age limit for people entering a long-term care facility. Though these vary; it makes sense to assume that people who need assistance in their activities of daily living or who are bed bound are most often retired. Let us assume that the people who will be residents in a long-term care facility are at least age sixty-five. I would like to share some information about people who are in the sixty-five and older age bracket that will help define their needs and the services they require.

In the early part of the twentieth century, the average life expectancy was about fifty years. The life expectancy in 1990 was about seventy-five years. In 1970 there were 203,982,310 people in the United States. Of that number, 20,097,490 were over the age of sixty-five. Of the people who were more than sixty-five, 1,430,010 were eighty-five years old or older. In the year 2,000, the population of the United States was 281,421,906. Of that number, 34,991,753 will be over the age of sixty-five, and 4,239,587 will be eighty-five years old or older. Those people who are more than sixty-five years old have nearly double between 1970 and 2,000. Those who are more than eighty-five have nearly tripled! By 2030, the estimated number of people over the age of sixty-five will be close to 70,000,000.[1]

One of the reasons for this increase in the average life expectancy is the tremendous strides that have been made in the field of medicine over the past century. We are able to do so much to prevent illness and to cure illnesses when they do occur. A second reason the life expectancy has increased by nearly twenty-five years has been better nutrition. We are keenly aware of our nutritional needs and have provided good support in programs like school lunches for our children and Meals on Wheels for our seniors. The final reason for increased longevity is better sanitation. Indoor plumbing, underground sewage and sewage treatment plants have helped to keep infections under check, and drinking water pure.

The implications of this situation are quite clear. Lower mortality and longer life expectancy mean that for the first time in human history, a society will exist wherein most of its members live to be old. This is good news for those who are aging, but we have, by virtue of this fact, created other problems. The United States Congress has, for several secessions, been struggling to decide how to ensure that Social Security will remain solvent once the "baby boomers" are in need of its benefits. Funds for Medicaid and Medicare will have to be increased in order to be able to meet the growing needs of the elderly. The typical "sandwich generation" children who once were working and in their forties or fifties when it came time to care for their parents are now closer to retirement age themselves, living on incomes that are substantially lower than they once were. The needs of the elderly will continue to grow.

When we talk about the older adult, it is imperative that we understand some things about that 65+ age group. This chapter will provide information on the physical condition of the elderly and some of the medical problems common to this age group. When we talk about an age group that goes from sixty-five to one hundred, it is obvious that not everyone has or will have the conditions listed below, but generally speaking, this will be an attempt to explain the most common ailments and diseases that afflict this age group. The intent here is to help the reader get a firm grasp of some limits the older adult might have as a result of physical decline and diseases common to the elderly. This knowledge will assist the long-term care administrator as they prepare to work with their residents.

There are several theories regarding why and how people age. They can be categorized into one of two general classes. The first class or groups of theories are called intrinsic, or "biological clock" theories. As the name may imply, the belief here is that we are biologically programmed to age the way we do. The programmed theories claim that the aging process is generated intentionally by the organisms from within (intrinsic), by the readout of a program, which is encoded within the DNA of the body's cells. Aging is seen in much the same way as the development and maturation of an individual. It is an extension of the normal developmental process, with some variation produced by interaction with one's environment. The general concept is that a biological clock is located somewhere in the body or in the cells, which at a certain time turns on or turns off specific genes leading to age-related changes in the body. Many people place this biological clock within the brain.

The second class of biological theories of aging are called the extrinsic, stochastic or "wear and tear" theories. These theories compare our bodies to that of a machine. The genes provide the body with a strong and viable physiology at about the time of sexual maturity. Over time, one's physiology degenerates due to normal unavoidable damage to body tissues, as well as to the abuse we heap upon ourselves. Ultimately, the accumulated damage causes failure of some critical biological system, and death results. In this theory, aging is a passive process, produced by internal and external agents, which cause damage to the body's systems.

It is easy to see the validity to both of these theories. There are some syndromes that have been identified that give great validity to the biological clock theory. The Hutchinson-Gilford syndrome and the Werner's syndrome are examples wherein people with these rare genetic mutations are doomed to a short life in which many of the hallmarks of advanced age occur very early in life. Yet, these cases are rare, and perhaps the more "normal" aging occurs as our bodies simply wear out over time.

There was a study done by Alexander Leaf, in "Scientific American", where he compared people who were 75 years old with persons who were 30 years old. He found in this study that those who were 75 years old had 92% of their former brain weight, 84% of their former basal metabolism, 70% of their former kidney filtration rate and 43% of their former maximum breathing capacity.[2] **What he is telling us with these statistics is that on average, when a person reaches age 75, their brain weighs 10% less, their body is burning calories at a reduced rate, their kidneys are filtering about three fourths as fast, and their lungs process oxygen more slowly. The implications of this information are that there is a slow down, decrease, or decline in the physical body as it ages.**

Generally speaking, though Leaf's data compares people age 30 to those age 75, aging is not a sudden event that happens at a certain age. It is, as one would assume, a gradual, continuous process that begins at birth. We know that at least some of the systems of the body decline at different rates in different individuals. They do however, decline in all people, from the point of their fullest development to a point where they have lost much of their abilities.

A study done by Kane, Ouslander and Abrass in 1989 indicates that under normal circumstances, the body rejects foreign cells, but as the body ages, there is a progressive weakening of the immune system. The result of this weakening is that the elderly become more susceptible to respiratory and other illnesses.[3] **For that reason, the elderly are encouraged to get flu shots each fall and tend to be more careful about colds and traveling, in bad weather.**

Choosing between these two classes of theories is less important than understanding the differences and being aware that no matter how we age, the fact remains that we do so. We all get old and as we do, our bodies change.

Physical Conditions

We know that at least some of the systems of the body decline at different rates in different individuals. They do however, decline in all people, from the point of their fullest development to a point where they have lost much of their abilities.

Under normal circumstances, the body rejects foreign cells, but as the body ages, there is a progressive weakening of the immune system. The result of this weakening is that the elderly become more susceptible to respiratory and other illnesses.

Listed below is a brief synopsis about the more common illnesses found in the elderly. Some of these are found in other age groups as well. In fact, many of the problems the elderly face are due to conditions of an earlier age. As people age, they often times find that they have needs that they can no longer meet on their own. Assistance from nursing professionals is required.

Cardiovascular Disease

Like the immune system mentioned above, that is affected by the ageing process, so too is the cardiovascular system affected. The degradation of the functional ability of the cardiovascular system usually interferes with the much-needed supply of nutrients and oxygen to the cells. As a result, the tissues and organs of the body are damaged. This damage leads eventually to the decline of other major processes.

As we age, we run a greater risk of cardiovascular diseases. These diseases include a wide range of disorders that may destroy the blood vessels of the heart. The combination of these diseases is the leading cause of death throughout the world. Such things as heredity, poor nutrition, and the environment may influence the disease.

When we talk about cardiovascular disease, we talk about two major types. The first is artery disease and the second is vein disease. The most significant cause of artery disease is the thickening and hardening of the artery walls by deposits of fatty materials. The second type, vein disease, involves the formation of blood clots. These clots usually form in the legs. Clots that form may break off and travel to the right side of the heart. From there, the clot may be pumped to the lung, but it gets trapped, as the pulmonary artery gets smaller. Once trapped, the clot may block or restrict the flow of blood to a portion of the lung creating a pulmonary infarction. The immediate shock may be fatal. Related to cardiovascular disease is heart disease. Most heart diseases are related to insufficient blood supply to the body tissues or overwork of the heart muscle. There are two kinds of heart diseases. They are either congenital or acquired. Congenital disorders result from abnormal development of the heart, but acquired disorders are due to heredity, environment and infectious processes that cause damage to the heart, the arteries, the valves or the conduction tissue.

The acquired disorders affect the elderly most often. In this case, the coronary arteries become blocked. That results in a lack of blood to the heart. Angina and shortness of breath usually result. If the blood flow to an area of the heart stops completely, heart muscle cells die. The result is what we commonly call a heart attack. The cells that have died form a scar and no longer function as a part of the heart muscle.

Some of the more common risk factors for coronary artery disease are: smoking, elevated cholesterol levels, obesity, hypertension and diabetes mellitus.

Cancer

In modern society, cancer is the second leading cause of death. Cancer has been known and described throughout history, although its greater prevalence today is certainly due to the conquest by medical science of most infectious diseases and to the increased life span of humans.

In the United States in the early 1990s more than one fifth of all deaths were caused by cancer. In 1993 the American Cancer Society predicted that about 33 percent of all Americans would eventually develop some form of the disease. Skin cancer is the most prevalent cancer in both men and women, followed by prostate cancer in men and breast cancer in women. Lung cancer, however, causes the most deaths in both men and women.

There are different types of cancer that affect the older adult. Below is just a bit of information about each. The first type of cancer to review is breast cancer. According to the American Cancer Society, breast cancer is the leading killer of women worldwide. The majority of cases occur in postmenopausal women. When breast cancer is diagnosed, treatment begins with surgical removal of the cancer. Most patients are then given radiation and/or chemotherapy treatments to make sure that all the cancer cells are destroyed. No one cause for breast cancer has been identified, but diet is believed to play a role.

Lung cancer is caused in most cases, by smoking. Cigarette smoke contains many initiating and promoting agents, placing at risk smokers and non-smokers who are regularly exposed to secondary smoke. Genetic factors may play some role in this disease since only about 20% of smokers develop lung cancer. By the time this cancer is diagnosed, the cancer has usually metastasized to the point where surgery, radiation and chemotherapy are not effective.

Prostate cancer is the second most common cancer in men. Unlike many other cancers, the incidence of prostate cancer increases dramatically with age; over 80% of all such cancers are diagnosed in men over the age of 65. Like breast cancer, early detection of prostate cancer is important. Unfortunately, the manual rectal examination is still one of the best ways to detect prostate cancer in older men. Treatment of this disease involves surgery, radiation and the use of hormones and chemotherapeutic drugs. The good news is that cancer prostate patients have excellent survival rates, exceeding 75%.

Skin cancer, one of the most common and preventable cancers, is usually caused by exposure to sunlight. The risk of developing skin cancer can be greatly decreased by limiting skin exposure to sunlight by wearing hats and light clothing or by using sun blocks to prevent the dangerous ultraviolet rays from damaging the skin. The most common types of skin cancer are readily diagnosed, treated, and cured at the early stages.

Cancer-causing agents, chemical, biological or physical, are termed carcinogen. Chemicals that cause cancer have a variety of molecular structures and include complex hydrocarbons, aromatic amines, and certain metals, drugs, hormones, and naturally occurring chemicals in molds and plants.

Sight

As we age, we experience more difficulty with our sight. In the long-term care facilities with which I have been affiliated; nearly 30% of the residents experience some kind of visual impairment, some of whom are totally blind. Nearly double that number, about 65% wear eyeglasses to correct their vision. For those residents, these facilities offered large print books from the library and ensured that menus were also printed in large print.

Lighting is also an issue of concern for the elderly. The glare from a nice shiny floor can present a problem. Older persons' eyes take longer to recover from glare than do those of a younger person. Adaptation to lighting levels, especially early-dark adaptation, takes longer for seniors because the lens of the eye thickens with age, causing less light to pass through and adaptation to be less flexible. A loss in accommodation, called presbyopia, decreases the ability for the eye to focus on close-up objects with age. The pupil diameter becomes smaller, causing less light to enter the eye. Cataracts cause a clouding of the lens and a decrease in the amount of light able to enter the eye. All of these normal changes to the eye as we age present a challenge to the elderly every day.

Another visual impairment to consider is the yellowing of the lens. As age increases, the lens of the eye not only thickens, but begins to yellow. The elderly person has difficulty discriminating among shorter wavelength colors and has better success with longer wavelengths. Reds and yellows are colors they can more easily discern. If we use a color contrast, the older eyes will not have as much difficulty.

Contrasts are very important to the elderly eye, especially while trying to navigate hallways that may not be light enough. If the floor is a light color, stairs should be a different color or have an edge that is a different color so the older person can easily distinguish that something different is about to happen here. Handrails or chair rails are also a tremendous help to persons with sight problems. Challenges with depth perception and diminished visual acuity cause difficulty in identifying stair height. Loss in stereopsis (depth perception) can cause problems in locomotion and way finding in the older individual. It is more difficult to walk quickly when suffering from the kinds of sight problems mentioned here.

Hearing

Poor sight is only one of the senses that decline as we age. Hearing is another of our senses that declines. The most common characteristic of an elderly person is that of someone who cannot hear. Presbycusis is a term used to describe any hearing impairment in old age, especially as it relates to high frequency tones.

An exercise that would help make the point would be for all those who work with the elderly to spend one day with some sound restricting material in their ears. Have them try to stay attentive to conversations. They will find in a hurry that it is easier to grin and nod their head than it is to keep up. I would suggest that at all meetings some kind of amplification be used so that everyone is able to hear.

Arthritis

For many elderly, arthritis is a condition they live with every day. Arthritis is an inflammation of a joint. There are several different kinds of arthritis but all have the affect of causing pain in the joint where it is found. It is most common in the fingers and knees, thus impeding locomotion and the use of hands.

Falls

70% of the deaths that result from falls occur with people age 65 and older. It is very easy to understand how this could happen. Older people living alone may fall down the steps, slip in the tub or fall and break a hip. In any long-term care facility, the highest safety priority is to prevent falls.

More than one third of people over the age of sixty-five experiences some form of fall related injury.[4] **It makes sense and is born out in evidence at any long-term care facility that the older one gets, the more susceptible they are to falls. A common problem among the elderly is orthostatic hypotension. This is simply being light headed when you rise from bed or chair too quickly. Often times this leads to dizziness that results in a fall. For the elderly who suffer from orthostatic hypotension, the best advice is to stand up slowly and stay standing for a few seconds before beginning to walk.**

Medication can also be a contributing factor in a fall. When a resident is admitted into a long-term care facility, a fall risk assessment should be done to alert the staff of the probability of a fall. Poor eyesight, an unsteady gate and confusion may also lead to falls.

Not all falls are due to the physical decline of the older resident. Some are due in part to the practice of putting the resident to bed soon after dinner. If a resident is asleep by 8:00 p.m., eight hours latter they are awake at 4:00 a.m. The night nurse believes it is too early for them to get up and encourages them to go back to bed. Since they are no longer tired, a sleeping pill is ordered to help them rest. Now, when they get up, they are even more unsteady than normal and are even more prone to fall.

One solution to assist residents besides paying attention to medications and practices is to institute an exercise program that helps them with muscle strengthening exercises. There are a variety of these programs available, but their advantage is that they provide strength, assist in balance and reduce the risk of falling. Moreover, a moderate exercise program may increase appetite and also act as a sleep aide.

Mental problems

One of the major brain related problems that seems to plague the older adult is the high risk of cerebrovascular accidents (CVA's), more commonly known as a stroke. The stroke is the most debilitating accident an elderly person can face. In the United States, 400,000 people have strokes annually, with one third dying from the insult. Strokes are the third leading cause of death. Many older adults suffer from strokes that have caused memory loss or paralysis. The cause of strokes is lack of oxygen to the brain. Blood carries the oxygen, so the lack of oxygen is usually the result of blockage of a major blood vessel called thrombotic strokes, or perhaps, the leakage of blood from a vessel that has ruptured, called hemorrhagic strokes. It is estimated that 60% of the cerebral vascular accidents are due to arterial thrombosis.

Some of the common results of a stroke may be aphasia, which is the inability to interpret and understand words, dysphasia, which deals more with the inability to speak and paralysis of one side of the body leaving the person unable to walk or use one arm.

Dementia is a term that broadly defines cognitive loss. Nearly half of all dementia are as a result of Alzheimer's disease. 20% of all dementia are due to multi infarcts, "mini strokes." Another 15% is a combination of Alzheimer' Disease and strokes. The remaining 15% is made up of other diseases like Parkinson's, Huntington's, Creutzfeldt—Jakole, Picks and depression.

Alzheimer's Disease, the largest cause of dementia, is a progressive brain disorder affecting memory, thought, behavior, personality and eventually, muscle control. It is estimated by the Alzheimer's Disease and Related Disorders Association, Inc. that the disease affects as many as four million Americans.

The Alzheimer's Association estimates that four million Americans have the disease. 10% of those adults over age 65 have the disease. 48% of those adults over age 85 have the disease. The Association states in its statistics sheet published in 1993 that Alzheimer's Disease is the fourth leading cause of death among adults.

Multi Infarct dementia is similar to Alzheimer's disease in that it produces a loss of intellectual function, but the reason for that loss is different. In this case, the loss is due to multiple strokes (infarcts) in the brain. These strokes may damage areas of the brain responsible for a specific function and can also produce generalized symptoms of dementia. Someone who suffers from multi-infarct dementia may be paralyzed on one side and display loss of memory or exhibit poor judgment.

Depression in the elderly is more common than many people believe. It is estimated that the lifetime risk for depressive disorder is on the order of 10-15 %. It is invoked by sadness, inactivity, loss of appetite, difficulty in thinking and concentration, feelings of hopelessness, and sometimes, suicidal tendencies. Depressed persons often have some mental deficits that include poor concentration and attention. Those who suffer from depression often times experience loss of memory of how to perform certain functions, the ability to recognize people they have known for years, and the ability to speak.

One of the potential problems depressed adults face is alcoholism. Those who are depressed often turn to alcohol as a means of self-medication. The stresses of aging with its losses and depression can lead to suicide or alcoholism. White males living alone and who are depressed are most likely to turn to alcohol. Those elderly who are both depressed and alcoholics are five times more likely to commit suicide.

The depression, which occurs without a precipitating event, is called endogenous depression. In its most severe form, it is virtually incapacitating. The victim losses the desire to get out of bed, eat, put on make up or shave. There is no motivation to do anything. In these cases, the intervention of a physician is necessary.

Clinical depression is a whole body disorder. It can affect the way you think as well as the way you feel, both physically and mentally. As many as three out of one hundred of people over the age of sixty-five suffer from clinical depression. It can be serious and in many cases, even result in suicide. The good news however is that nearly 80% of the people with clinical depression can be treated successfully. Even the most serious depressions can be managed with the right combinations of medication and the therapy.

Not everyone over the age of sixty-five will suffer from all of the physical and mental conditions mentioned above, but many of the people who move into assisted living facilities and nursing homes will suffer from one or more of them. Being aware of the problems will help prepare to meet the needs and to have realistic expectations of the residents when planning meals and activities or designing a new facility.

Chapter Two

Dealing with Loss

The happy retirement years that everyone looks forward to are not always so happy. During those retirement years, we also find that the elderly suffer many losses. There is a loss of income, and so, a change in life style. There is a loss of identity. Most men identify themselves with their work. After retirement, there is a loss of identity, and in some cases, a loss of worth or value. When you consider the age of the person, it becomes plain that those over age 65 suffer many losses in the years that remain of their lives. It is most often that one's parents die, if they have not already, when their children are in this retirement age. In the normal progression, spouses who have not already will also die during this time frame. And, though it is less common, many times parents in their older years suffer the loss of their children through disease or accident. Though retirement may be a time to move to a warmer climate, such a move brings with it the loss of a house, a home, and a space that is full of memories. The loss of health is another loss commonly endured by the elderly. As we have already discussed, with the physical decline may also come mental decline. These losses, along with all those that have already been mentioned, produce stress, grief and anxiety.

When a person's health declines to the point that they must enter a long-term care facility, unless it is for short-term therapy, most people assume the move is the last one they will make. For many people, this is true. Perhaps that is why it is resisted so much. Unfortunately, most often, the elderly enter the facility directly from the hospital because it has been determined by the physician or their family that they can no longer live independently. They suffer many losses upon admission to a facility that effect their feelings and behavior.

The first loss, of course, is the loss of familiar surroundings. Often times the elderly have lived in their current home for twenty years or more. Their homes are filled with furniture they have accumulated and used for forty years. Favorite pictures and easy chairs have made their house a home. Memories surround every piece of furniture, every cracked dish, every pair of slippers or sweater sent for father's day and mother's day over the years. To leave home is a major life adjustment. It means leaving so much of oneself, against one's will, to go to a new unfamiliar place. It means adopting oneself and one's life style from living in an eight room house to only one room.

A second loss that is encountered when an elderly person enters a long-term care facility is the loss of family contact. The family does not feel as free to drop by to visit any more. Without the extra bedrooms, it becomes expensive for the family to visit who live out of the area. As a result, they come by less often than they did before. When they do come to visit, the room is too small for everyone to sit in and there are usually only one or two extra chairs for guests. As the elderly person becomes frailer and in firmed, they may require medical attention or become confused and the family members feel less and less comfortable coming to visit.

Often times, families of demented residents find it very difficult to visit because the resident no longer identifies them as a spouse or child. They are not the person they used to be. Their personality has changed. Their behavior can be embarrassing. The family gets fewer rewards out of visiting and simply stops coming.

A third loss suffered by those who are institutionalized is the loss of contact with friends. Usually, by the time someone is admitted to the assisted living facility or nursing home, they are past retirement age. The average age of those in the nursing home where I worked is 85. Most of their friends are the same age. They too are frail and elderly and do not usually get out to visit. When they do, what they see in the facility reminds them that they too could and may be in a similar situation.

The fourth loss experienced by every person who enters a long-term care facility is the loss of control over his/ her life. Life in a facility is run on a schedule. There are times to get up, eat, take medication, participate in activities and take a bath. The more incapacitated one becomes, the less options are given to them. Doctors and nursing staff dictate what will be done when and in what manner. Food that had been prepared a certain way for forty years is now being prepared by someone else who does it in a different way. Routines that have been developed over the years are now changed to meet the routine of the facility.

Perhaps the hardest part of living in a facility is sharing a room with someone. Going from a house to a room is bad enough, but having to share that room with someone else is even harder. There is no privacy and room for very few personal things. The things that help establish our identity and remind us of our past are gone. It is indeed hard.

In addition to the other losses mentioned above, some people also suffer from physical losses that precipitate this institutionalization. Hip replacements due to severe arthritis, leg amputation due to circulation problems and sugar diabetes, strokes and accidents bring the elderly to a long-term care facility. Some are there for a short time, but for many, this kind of placement is most appropriate. If you couple loss of home with loss of limb, it is easy to see that the elderly in this situation need an extra amount of attention and support.

It seems that there are at least six major types of loss. Those mentioned above can be placed into one or another of these types of loss.

The first is material loss; the loss of a physical object or of familiar surroundings to which one has an important attachment. Leaving a house one has lived in for many years to go to an assisted living facility or a nursing home can create this kind of loss. The second kind of loss is relationship loss; the ending of opportunities to relate oneself, to talk with, share experiences with, make love to, be in touch, settle issues with, argue with, and otherwise be in the emotional or physical presence of a particular human being. It is easy to see how those over age 65 can face this kind of loss with their parents, spouses, children and friends. A third kind of loss is intra psychic loss; losing an important image of oneself, losing the possibility of what might have been, abandonment of plans for a particular future, the dying of a dream. This is entirely an inward experience. How often have we heard people say that when they retire they will do one thing or another, only to have plans changed due to circumstances not planned on earlier? It may be his or her own physical health that fails, or responsibilities to provide care for a parent. Their dreams are unfulfilled, and so they grieve. The fourth kind of loss is functional loss; loss of one of the muscular or neurological functions of the body. Strokes, heart attacks, cancer, diabetes all cause this kind of loss. Strokes that cause the loss of the use of speech or limbs are very difficult for people to accept. Role loss is the fifth kind of loss. This is when one experiences the loss of a specific social role of one's accustomed place in a social network. We have talked about retirement as an example of this kind of loss. But often times, when our spouse dies, we no longer feel comfortable in our circle of friends who are still couples. The last kind of loss is systemic loss. This loss is the destruction of the system, that is, family, work or government. Death of a spouse or loved one can change a system like no other. We all have known couples where each performs certain tasks. Upon the death of one spouse, the system breaks down. The remaining person from the couple has to develop a new system.

Along with the various kinds of losses identified above, there are other variables loss may include. There is the avoidable and the unavoidable loss, the temporary and the permanent loss, the actual and the imagined loss, the anticipated and the unanticipated loss and finally, leaving and being left. By thinking through these variations and being aware of them, the long-term care administrator will better understand the situation in which many residents find themselves.

Perhaps the biggest or hardest loss people who are sixty-five and older will face is the death of a spouse. Of course, it is easy to imagine that this is true. If we take this a step farther, we also know that the average age at which people die in our country for both men and women falls within this 65 plus age group we have been talking about. For that reason, it is important to pay particular attention to the loss caused by death presented in the following paragraphs.

When we consider death as loss, we must begin with understanding of terms. Grief is the emotional, behavioral reaction of the person who suffers the loss. Bereavement is the reconciliation or perhaps the integration of this loss in our lives. It is a process that follows grieving. The reconciliation takes place a little at a time until finally, we are able to say that we are over the grieving and have accepted the hurt that accompanies loss. Mitchell and Anderson, in their book, *All Our Losses/ All Our Griefs* say that grief is universal, inescapable, even when its existence and impact are denied. It is a composite of powerful emotions confronting us when we lose someone or something we value. It is the work we engage in that enables us to eventually live full, satisfying lives.[5]

There are certain dynamics of grief. Grief emotions tend to be grouped into five different clusters. The first of these emotions is emptiness. This may include loneliness or isolation. When we feel empty, we feel somehow diminished from within. Loneliness is the sense that one's surroundings are also empty of any of the people who matter or care. Isolation is the sense of being divided from others by some invisible boundary. A second dynamic of grief is fear and anxiety. Prior to the anticipated death of a loved one, we may feel the dread of abandonment. Afterward, we experience the anxiety of separation. We ask ourselves, "What am I ever going to do without him/her?"

The third dynamic of grief deals with guilt and shame. As you can imagine, guilt is a dominant component of grief. We feel guilty when we assume responsibility for the loss, made decisions that may have in some way hastened the loss or have not had an opportunity to resolve hurt feelings in our relationship with the person who has died. Anger is the fourth dynamic of grief. When the loss is death, the anger is often times directed at other family members, medical personnel or God. Sadness and despair are also dynamics we see often in grief. It is normal to feel sad over the loss of something. The degree of sadness is usually equal to the kind of loss. But when sadness is coupled with a sense of futility about the future, that is despair. When people find themselves in a state of despair, psychological intervention is necessary quickly. When an older person is left alone due to the death of a spouse, they sometimes give up, thinking they have no reason to go on. These dynamics of grief can be found in small or large degree depending on the loss and the circumstances of it. When we think about the elderly and death, once again, they will suffer more from loss than any other age group. Helping them deal with these losses should be a priority of the social worker and chaplain in the facility.

The major dynamic of the inner experience of grief is that of anxiety. All of the behavioral responses that we observe in grief, including fear, seem to be related to anxiety. If anxiety is the perception of a threat to ourselves, then it is easy to see how it relates to fear. Being in a situation similar to one that caused harm or discomfort earlier produces some anxiety. Just remembering the discomfort brought on the anxiety.

Nearly everyone felt some sort of separation anxiety when we went off to school or summer camp or college. We were anxious because we were not sure what the new experience would bring. We did know what we had and how to function in it. The same would be true regarding death. Our anxiety would be the fear of not knowing what was going to happen next, or how we would cope. Questions arise at funerals that indicate that perhaps for the first time, people are asking about life after death, the nature of God and who and what they are compared to other forms of existence. Death does make us pause to contemplate, and in that contemplation, feel anxious about not only the person who died but about ourselves and what might become of us.

Though emptiness, guilt and anger are dynamics of grief, it does seem clear that anxiety is prevalent throughout our struggle with grief.

Some twenty-five years ago Elizabeth Kubler-Ross wrote a book called *On Death and Dying*. It began an open and frank discussion about death, preparing for death and dealing with the death of a loved one. There have been many other authors who have suggested similar stages of death and dying. I was fortunate to hear a lecture by Dr. Alan Wolfelt, who directs the Center for Loss and Life Transition, on this topic. He identified three stages of grief. The first was what he called the "evasion of the new reality." In this stage the person goes through the normal reactions to death: shock, denial, numbness. The normal reactions tend to help us protect ourselves against the horrible shock of accepting that one we knew and loved is dead. I have seen many parishioners go through this stage of grief. I have been by their side as they watched their mate die. In long-term care facilities, most often one spouse has already died before the survivor comes to the assisted living community or nursing home, but sometimes we are fortunate to have couples living together or to have single people find each other and marry within the building

The second stage Dr. Wolfelt identifies is called "encounter with new reality." Here people become anxious, panic and are fearful because they are beginning to realize what the death will mean for their own lives. One might express explosive emotions or be irrational in blaming themselves. They may feel guilt, remorse, loss, emptiness or sadness. I knew a lady whose husband died. She got through the first stage of shock and denial, but them she began to blame herself for his death because she allowed him to eat fatty foods and to sit around rather than exercise in any way. She was the classic "turtle" that blamed herself for his ill health. This is the time when questions about eternal life come up. The questions may be regarding the deceased but may also be asked as a way of reassuring oneself.

In the final stage, Dr. Wolfelt indicates that "reconciliation to the new reality" takes place. In this stage, one may feel some relief, or release; a sense of letting go. Finally there is reconciliation, acceptance. Most people get to this point. Memorial services when a resident dies is one way of helping the residents there who could not get to the normal funeral service. Visits to residents in the facility, to listen to the thoughts and fears of going on alone, are a good way to assist those who have gone through the shock and anxiety associated with grief. Many long-term care facilities have social workers or chaplains who can make these visits, but a visit from the administrator sends a clear message of care and compassion.

Reconciliation is a process that takes time. It is not an event that occurs suddenly. How long it takes for someone to move to the point of reconciliation is unique for each person. Special occasions like holidays, anniversaries and birthdays may trigger a resurgence of feelings that the person thought they had worked through.

Understanding the types of losses residents may endure will help the administrator better plan for programs or services that will assist the facility in meeting the needs. Being able to understand the needs will help justify the expenditure of time and money to meet those needs.

Chapter Three

Spiritual Needs

In addition to understanding the physical and psychological make up of older adults, it is also important to understand the spiritual dimension of their lives. Everyone has spiritual needs. Dr. Harold Koenig, in his book, Aging and God, defines spiritual needs as a "conscious or unconscious striving that arise from the influence of the human spirit on the biopsychosocial natures. They are a consequence of an inherent human impulse to relate to God, and also reflect God's influence on and desire to relate to humanity. Spiritual needs stem from a recognition that human life is finite and that there is a higher purpose to which people are called."[6] Those who are older or medically ill are confronted by the reality that they may die. Those who are healthy may be able to ignore concerns about death or life after death, but when one has been told by their physician that there is nothing more they can do, some of the fourteen needs Doctor Koenig identifies come readily to the surface.

These fourteen spiritual needs are: 1.The need for meaning, purpose and hope. 2. The need to transcend circumstances. 3. The need for support in dealing with loss. 4. The need for continuity. 5. The need for validation and support of religious behaviors. 6. The need to engage in religious behaviors. 7. The need for personal dignity and sense of worthiness. 8. The need for unconditional love. 9. The need to express anger and doubt. 10. The need to feel that God is on their side. 11. The need to love and serve others. 12. The need to be thankful. 13. The need to forgive and be forgiven. 14. The need to prepare for death and dying.[7]

The need for meaning, purpose and hope is fundamental in life. Most older adults struggle with meaning as they age. Life has to have been spent on something. As older people approach death either due to physical illness or simply by virtue of having lived a long life, they need some assurance that life has been for something, that life has meaning and purpose, that their struggles have been worth the effort. Those who are religious hang on to the hope that there is more to life than the pain and suffering they may be currently experiencing. If death is eminent, the hope is for an after life. In some cases, illness and suffering may be seen as God testing a person, or the will of God. Depending upon what one believes, their faith, may inspire them and provide them with purpose to fight on another day.

The second spiritual need, to transcend circumstances, can be seen in many examples. Someone who is dying of cancer may get to the point where they are no longer concerned about themselves, but are able to get beyond their own condition to contemplate the hereafter. Their faith inspires them to move on in spite of their immediate circumstances.

The third need, for support in dealing with loss, is, as identified in the last chapter, one of the spiritual needs the elderly face. Most often parents die before their children are sixty-five. But if the parents have not died by the time the children retire, the chance of them doing so before the children is quite good. The elderly face death often. Besides their parents, sometimes their children die. Many times their friends die. People who are elders face these many losses as they age.

The fourth spiritual need Dr. Koening identifies is the need for continuity. This is true for all people, but especially for the elderly who are suffering from some form of dementia. The structure and order helps those who are having a difficult time with memory continue to function on their own.

When you think about continuity, review your own daily routine. I imagine you can recite step by step how you get up and get ready for the day. We are most comfortable when we operate out of a routine. We set the routine based on our likes and dislikes and follow the routine because in doing so, we are comfortable. We follow the same route to work and stop at the same gas stations to buy our gasoline and morning cup of coffee.

Lack of continuity, as in a move from home to a retirement community, can produce transfer trauma. Transfer trauma is the physical and emotional changes that come from loss. One of the losses we face when we go to a hospital or long-term care community is the loss of control.

One of the most reassuring things we find in our religious faith is our understanding that God will be there for us whenever needed. People from the Judeo-Christian background believe that God is the beginning and the end, the alpha and omega. This understanding helps to keep us centered in the face of distress.

The fifth spiritual need is for validation and support of religious behaviors. The older person may find activities like daily prayers, scripture reading or meditation helpful to them in coping with the stresses they face. By validating the use of this religious behavior, the older adult will be reaffirmed.

The sixth spiritual need is the need to engage in religious behavior. Bible study, prayer and scripture reading are examples of important religious behavior. Prayer buddies that phone one another and pray together are very important and are an activity that the elderly can be involved in easily. The residents in a long-term care community could easily be a part of this kind of activity by phone if their church had a speakerphone of some sort that would enable them to be a part of the conversation. They can be involved in bible study by phone, tape or videotape. It is possible to have a mid day bible study and lunch for the over 65 group that would feed the body and the soul.

The seventh spiritual need is for personal dignity and sense of worthiness. Scared from surgery, deformed from a stroke, confused from dementia; older adults can easily lose their sense of dignity. Being dependent upon someone else to feed you and change your diaper can cause a negative affect on how you feel about yourself. In light of the fact that bodies do decline as we age, how can we help the elders feel worthy? Is this not a place where clergy or chaplains can talk to the older adult about grace and love?

The eighth spiritual need is for unconditional love. All people need to feel loved. They need acceptance and forgiveness. As we age we look back at our lives and begin to take stalk. We wonder how someone so sinful can be given grace and unconditional love. It is hard for us to accept this kind of love.

The ninth spiritual need is the need to express anger and doubt. When we are afflicted by a serious illness or when our spouse dies, there is a natural tendency to blame God, or at least to ask why this happened. Many people blame God when bad things happen to them. Others blame themselves. Sometimes those people who blame God end up feeling guilty for having done so. All of us need to feel comfortable enough with our God that we can voice what is in our hearts, be that anger, sadness or doubt.

The tenth spiritual need is to feel that God is on our side. After we get angry at God and doubt God's ability or existence, many times we get to the point where we come to the realization that God is on our side. Similar to the stages of grief, we go through a process, often times, when we are diagnosed with a terminal illness and need to get to the point of acceptance. In this case we get angry, we express doubt and finally we get to the point were we can say, "Okay, what is happening is not what I want, but with your help God, I'll get through it." Often times it takes a major event of some sort to get us to the point where we begin to depend upon God and know for sure that God is with us, no matter what.

The eleventh spiritual need is to love and serve others. This comes as a direct result of knowing that others love us, including our God. When we feel loved, we naturally want to express our love as well. It is an amazing thing. The more we share of ourselves, the better we feel about it. Don't we all feel good when we have done a good deed? This is true of the elderly. The older they get the more useless they feel. Their training and expertise is quickly outdated. They are no longer the president of this or that, but the past president. Their physical abilities decline and they no longer have the stamina they used to have.

The twelfth spiritual need is the need to be thankful. I do not believe that there is a greater need in our spiritual development than the need to feel thankful. It is easy to get down. It is easy to feel sorry for ourselves. It is easy to see the glass half empty. But, moaning about our problems, dwelling on the negative and seething in anger about one thing or another never gets us out of the muck and back onto the road to acceptance of our situation.

The thirteenth spiritual need is the need to forgive and to be forgiven. I am always amazed at the people who go to their grave holding a grudge against someone else. I am amazed at the families where one sibling does not speak to another. I am amazed at the number of people who have made a mistake and are too proud to go to the person they have offended to seek forgiveness.

The fourteenth spiritual need is the need to prepare for death and dying. The assurance we can give the older adult is that this life is not all there is. The hope of an afterlife will sustain them during illnesses and give them hope.

Understanding these fourteen spiritual needs offered to us by Dr. Koenig can serve the administrator well as he/she works with the elderly. Sharing this information with the activities staff or the chaplain will enable the community to support the residents who are struggling with through any of these fourteen spiritual needs.

Part Two
Administration

Chapter Four

Administration

Now that basic information has been shared regarding the physical, emotional and spiritual needs of the elderly, I would like to discuss how long-term care facilities might manage themselves to meet these needs. This chapter deals with administration in general. The next four deal with the importance of a management plan, communication, the use of a quality assurance/quality improvement program as a management tool and customer service. The chapters following these two will offer a closer examination of purpose and function of the various departments typically found in a long-term care facility. In a typical training program, a new administrator would work with each department to understand the regulations they are required to follow and to see how each relates to the others to help provide the care the residents require. Let us begin with an overview of administration.

James E. Allen identifies the following nine areas as the responsibilities of management: forecasting, planning, organizing, staffing, directing, evaluating, controlling, innovating and marketing. He explains that forecasting is projecting trends or needs that must be met in the future. Planning is described as deciding what needs to be done and setting forth a plan of how to accomplish it. Organizing, according to Allen, is deciding how to structure a suitable organization to implement the plan. Staffing is finding the right person for the job. Directing includes training and supervision that explains to the employees what is expected of them. Evaluating is determining how well the organization is accomplishing its goals. By controlling, the administrator makes sure the goals are being accomplished and the jobs are being done correctly. The innovative administrator leads the staff to think creatively about how to make the facility more attractive. Marketing assures that the facility will be successful by attracting the kind of residents it is designed to serve.[8] The remainder of this chapter will look at these responsibilities to various degrees while also introducing additional information to help the administrator understand the assisted living industry and his/ her role in it.

1. Forecasting

Forecasting is predicting what might happen that could impact on the facility. This cannot simply be a guess. To be able to accurately forecast, the administrator must review pertinent information. By being aware of census data in a facility over the past ten years, the administrator will know if the potential for continual growth exists in the facility. Knowing the same information about one's competitors will provide a wider few of the community and not simply one's own facility. Being aware of what is happening economically in the city where the facility is located will also help determine the ability of future residents to pay a given rate. Anticipating government funding for certain people or programs enables the administrator to begin to make the decisions necessary to meet the changes anticipated.

2. Planning

Planning is an essential function of administration. It enables the business to work toward a goal, to make decisions based on where it wants to be in a year as opposed to simply reacting to the pressures of business.

Planning begins with a mission statement. The statement should identify in a few sentences what your purpose is for existing. What does the facility want to accomplish? The statement may say something like, "We would like to provide a warm, friendly and safe environment for the elderly where medical, social and spiritual needs may be met." This becomes the cornerstone for the goals that are set and for decisions made in the future.

Once the mission is defined, the next step in planning is to determine how the facility will accomplish this mission. For this step goals are established. A goal is something to work toward that will help fulfill the mission. Assuming that the mission statement above is the mission statement for the facility where you work, the goals that are set should enable that facility to fulfill the mission. The question to be answered is how will this facility provide a warm, friendly safe environment for the elderly where medical, social and spiritual needs are met? The goals should say how something will be done, who is going to do it, when it will be accomplished and how much it will cost.

One goal may be that the administrator will establish hiring policies within three months that require that personality be considered when selecting future staff members. A second goal may be that the administrator will establish a safety committee that will review all current practices, and will evaluate the living environment to determine how the facility could be as safe as possible for the residents.

When the goals are established, the next step is to determine how the goals will be accomplished. What will happen? When will it happen? Who will be responsible? How much will this cost?

Fulfilling the goals may cost money. It is important that the planning be done prior to establishing a budget. They are certainly not the only items in the budget, but if there are expenses identified, these expenses need to be budgeted so as not to adversely affect current operating expenses.

A final note regarding planning is that the marketing plan is also a part of this process. The market plan should be completed based on what the goals of the community are as set during this planning stage. The market plan will be discussed later in the marketing chapter.

3. Organizing

Organizing and reorganizing are similar. They require experience and a clear knowledge of what needs to be accomplished. By forecasting and planning, the administrator is then able to begin to put a structure together to make the plan work. Organizing includes deciding on how much staff is necessary and how they will relate to one another. One of the results of this effort is an organizational chart that shows how positions relate to one another. In the following example it is clear that the administrator supervises Department Directors who in turn supervise others.

Organizational Chart for the #1 long-term care facility

Board of Directors
Administrator
Department Directors
Assistant Department Directors
Supervisors
Line Staff

In the Nursing department, for example, it might look like this:

Director of Nursing
Assistant Director of Nursing

Administrative Nurses
Supervisors
Licensed practical nurses
Certified nurse aides

In the Dining Department it might look like this:

Director of Dining Services
Food Service manager
Tray line supervisor
Wait Staff supervisor
Chefs
Cooks
Prep cooks
Kitchen aides

Each department will have at least a director and one other employee. The directors all report to the administrator and all the people in their department report to them.

Nursing homes also have physical, occupational, and speech therapists either on staff or under contract to perform their particular duties. A dietitian is also required as a full or part time staff member. In addition, a physician is required to serve as the medical director. Other physicians like dentists, podiatrists and optometrists are also required to provide the services required by this elderly population.

An additional part of organization is policies that tell employees what is expected of them. Having written policies explaining how something is to occur insures continuity of care or service no matter who is providing that care. Policies should be clear. There should follow each policy a procedure written out that explains in detail the steps required in following the policy. The following example will help make the point.

Policy Title: Employee Clock in
Department: Administration

Policy: It is the responsibility of all hourly employees to clock in and out using the time clock located at the rear entrance.

Procedure: Hourly employees will find their time card located in the rack on the right side of the time clock. Follow these steps to clock in and out.
1. Insert the time card into the time clock until it clicks.
2. Remove the time card and check to see that the clock has stamped the correct time on the card.
3. Replace the card in the rack.
4. To clock out at the end of the shift, repeat steps one through three above.
Date of policy:_____
administrator's signature:_____
These two suggestions are examples of how to organize the facility to best meet the goals that have been set during the planning stage.

4. Staffing
Staffing will be covered under the chapter on human resources, however, a quick note here will help the administrator with many important decisions regarding who is hired to fill the organizational needs. It is important to know what kind of person is needed for each job. A director of nursing should be someone who has experience in long-term care. The director of marketing person should be a positive, outgoing, knowledgeable, cheerful person. The director of maintenance should have general skills that enable him to recognize problems with equipment as well as the ability to make minor repairs. But most importantly, the administrator needs to be able to get along with them and they need to be able to get along with each other. I recommend that the administrator hire those people who report directly to him/her and allow the department directors to do the same.
There are those who live by the adage that you should hire the right person and then find them a job in the organization. There is merit to this school of thought in many ways. The question is what qualities are you looking for in the right person? Do you want all nurses to be compassionate? Are all employees to be cheerful? Is a well-organized person your ideal employee? Is the right person the one who compensates for your weakness or the one who compliments you on your haircut?

5. Directing
Directing is oversight. It is taking care of the day-to-day problems that arise. Often times this comes in the form of helping the staff grow into their job, encouraging someone to do better, or disciplining others who will not.

Providing in-service training is an essential part of helping staff members grow into their positions. Many different in-service training opportunities exist outside the facility, but quick five-minute in-services that explain how something is to be done or to introduce a new policy can be very beneficial. The administrator is the one person responsible for everything that happens in the facility. Directing the rest of the staff is a major part of his/her job.

6. Evaluating

Like staffing above, evaluating will be discussed in greater detail in the chapter on human resources. But, evaluating employees is only part of the job of the administrator. He/she will also need to evaluate how things are going, and why they are going the way they are. This includes finances, staff moral, resident census and satisfaction. One way to get this kind of feedback is through surveys that the administrator will ask residents, families or staff members to complete on one topic or another. Financial statements also give the administrator much needed information.

7. Controlling

The result of evaluations leads to decisions on what needs to change to get the facility on track or keep it on track. This is a good opportunity to introduce a quality assurance program. You will find details about quality assurance and quality improvement later in this chapter. For now, it is important to say that once a problem is identified, it is appropriate to ask what can be done to fix it. Coming up with that answer and making the changes necessary is what controlling is all about.

8. Innovating

Some people are innovative in that they can think of new ideas or new ways of doing things. Others are not. If the administrator is not innovative, it is wise to hire department directors who are or to attend in-service training or to develop a rapport with colleagues in the business so that ideas can be shared and solutions suggested. If the administrator is new to long-term care, it may be a good idea to find an older successful administrator to use as a mentor. It may also be good to seek the advice of a volunteer board that is willing to give feedback and help advise the administrator on issues he/she would bring before them.

9. *Marketing*

Marketing is selling the community. An entire chapter is devoted to this important aspect of the administrator's job.

The administrator of any long-term care facility is the person in charge. He or she is responsible for everything that happens there. Allen has identified the responsibilities of a leader. Now, it would be good to discuss a little about the characteristics of an effective leader.

Katz and Kahn, in their book entitled, *The Social Psychology of Organizations*, have indicated that an effective leader is one who:

1. Reconciles what needs to be accomplished to the needs of the employees to the end that the organization benefits. What needs to be done in a long-term care facility is pretty basic. People need food, medical attention, socialization and inspiration. Employees need to fell like what they do makes a difference. They need to be recognized and appreciated. They need a stable fulfilling work environment where they are shown respect regardless of their level of income or the work they perform.

2. Encourages both group and personal loyalty.

3. Shows that he cares about the employees.

4. Depends on the respect he gets from the employees because of what he does rather than who he is.

5. Encourages the employees to be proud of where they work.

6. Creates commitment to the organization among the employees.[9]

One of the ways to determine if an administrator is effective is to look at employee satisfaction. The administrator and the department directors taking a personal interest in the lives of the employees can promote facility loyalty and dedication. Pride in work is created through positive surveys from an oversight organization and positive outcomes with healing, recovery or perhaps a letter of thanks shared with the staff.

Sydney Finkelstein, in his book *,Why Smart Executives Fail and What We Can Learn From Their Mistakes* indicates that one of the best ways to succeed is to have open communication with employees. "Openness means fighting the natural tendency to cover up unfavorable or distasteful information. It requires leaders to set the standard for learning from mistakes-an unnatural act in many organizations. Leaders who are unable or unwilling to build a culture of openness create organizations that almost choose not to learn. They are defensive, not open."[10] To be open requires accessibility. It requires that the administrator get from behind the desk and onto the floors.

It requires a means for employees to share thoughts, concerns or questions. Getting to know the employees personally fosters both communication and shows the employees that the administrator cares about them as people.

Even if the administrator gets good information and feedback from the employees and residents, it may be hard to change a mindset that is entrenched in a facility. Roadblocks come up when a reduction in staff is proposed or a change in the way "we have always done it" is suggested. But, there are ways around these obstacles. In the book *Execution, the Discipline of Getting Things Done*, Larry Bossidy and Ram Charan say that to create cultural change, you simply need to change people's behavior so they produce results. They identify three steps to make this happen. "First you tell people clearly what results you're looking for. Then you discuss how to get those results, as a key element of the coaching process. Then you reward people for producing the results. If they come up short, you provide additional coaching, withdraw rewards, give them other jobs, or let them go. When you do these things, you create a cultural of getting things done."[11]

Department directors are the people who most often report to the administrator. The place to begin to make change is with this group. By following the three-step advice, change will begin to occur. The administrator then needs to stand behind the Department Director as he/she implements the same sort of administrative strategy within their departments.

Efficient, effective and economical

Every administrator makes numerous decisions each day. When making these decisions, the administrator should consider the short-term and long-term impact of the decision. One very helpful way to do that is to quickly ask if the decision being made will help the facility run more efficiently, effectively and economically.

Efficiency is the ability to produce the desired effect with the minimum effort. For an organization, the challenge is to get the maximum amount accomplished with the minimum effort. It relates to the common saying that one needs to work smarter not harder.

Effectiveness is the ability to accomplish what you set out to do. Achieving the desired effect, meeting the goal, completing the job are examples of effectiveness.

Economical is not wasting money, time, fuel etc.

A good leader is able to get a job done with minimal effort at the lowest cost. If one were only concerned about efficiency, producing the desired effect with the minimum effort, and not economy, the business could easily lose money and close the doors. If one were only concerned about getting the job done, regardless of the effort or expense, the business might once again lose money and close the doors. If one were only concerned about the cost and not about the accomplishment, the service provided would suffer and the public would decide that it is time to close the door.

Juggling these three balls is the job of the leader. The employees will always say they need more help, more employees, but more employees cost more money and having a 3 to 1 ratio of residents to staff may not be very efficient. Cutting expenses too far might lead to the inability to meet the desired goal of providing good quality care. Every component of long-term care has been around long enough to have established a good benchmark for how many nurse aides to use to provide good care to a certain number of residents in either assisted living or nursing home care. The other long-term care facilities nearby can provide a salary range for employees so that you are not paying too much or too little. Pay attention to what your competitors are doing so that you do not get left behind. By using these three E's, (effective, efficient, economical) in making decisions, you will make your community the community of choice for both employees and residents.

One final comment on management deals with leadership styles. Jim Collins, in his book, *Good to Great*, indicated that one of the surprising results of his research in identifying those companies that had moved from being a good company to a great company was that the type of leadership required most often was not the high-profile leaders with big personalities who made headlines and became celebrities. No, the leaders who moved good companies to become great companies were self-effacing, quiet, reserved, even shy. The were "the paradoxical blend of personal humility and professional will."[12] Good leaders who do not work out of a motive to feed their own ego or meet their own needs, but put the needs of the community and residents above their own will be the most successful leaders in the long run.

The administrator must always act within the bonds of his/her authority. There is a role to be played. Part of that role includes accountability for the facility and how well it meets federal, state and local regulations. Terms like "in good faith" and "with the care an ordinary prudent person in a similar situation would use," indicates that the administrator is responsible and will be held responsible for their actions. The board or a management company that works for the board normally hires the administrator. This implies that they answer to the board and can by fired by the board. Overstepping the limits of responsibility is an easy way to get in trouble with the board. The job of the administrator is to implement the mission and policy statements. In so doing the general direction set by the board is followed. In addition, he /she must operate as the overseer of the entire facility, making sure that regulations, laws and policies are all honored in the process.

The job of the administrator, at whatever level, is full of responsibilities. It requires that one knows how to deal with residents, families, employees and contract employees. It also requires that one is knowledgeable of the numerous regulations as well as how best to encourage employees to adhere to them every day. The following chapters will help prepare the administrator to do these things and much more, but first, I would like to share some of the responsibilities as they relate to federal nursing home regulations found in the Code of Federal Regulations.

Sec. 483.75 Administration.

A facility must be administered in a manner that enables it to use its resources effectively and efficiently to attain or maintain the highest practicable physical, mental, and psychosocial well being of each resident.

(a) Licensure. A facility must be licensed under applicable state and local law.

(b) Compliance with federal, state, and local laws and professional standards. The facility must operate and provide services in compliance with all applicable federal, state, and local laws, regulations, and codes, and with accepted professional standards and principles that apply to professionals providing services in such a facility.

(c) Relationship to other Health and Human Services regulations. In addition to compliance with the regulations set forth in this subpart, facilities are obliged to meet the applicable provisions of other Health and Human Services regulations, including but not limited to those pertaining to nondiscrimination on the basis of race, color, or national origin (45 CFR part 80); nondiscrimination on the basis of handicap (45 CFR part 84); nondiscrimination on the basis of age (45 CFR part 91); protection of human subjects of research (45 CFR part 46); and fraud and abuse (42 CFR part 455). Although these regulations are not in themselves considered requirements under this part, their violation may result in the termination or suspension of, or the refusal to grant or continue payment with federal funds."[13]

The administrator must be very knowledgeable of not only the federal regulations, but also the state and local regulations. Learning these regulations will enable the long-term care administrator to better direct the staff and ensure that the facility stays in compliance with everything from local fire codes and health department regulations to federal regulations. All of these are important. Knowledge of them will enable the administrator to pass along that knowledge to department directors so that they can train the members of their departments. Policies can be based upon meeting or exceeding these regulations. Goals can be set to operate the facility in such a manner as to be deficiency free from one inspection to another. Employee evaluations can be based in part on how they helped to meet these goals. But it all begins with the administrator and the knowledge they have of all of the regulations that pertain to their business.

Chapter Five

Management Plan

Using these various responsibilities as outlined in the previous chapter, the administrator will be in a position to prepare a management plan. The management plan will provide the road map for the future of the facility. By virtue of making this plan, the administrator will be compelled to think through a number of issues that will better prepare him/her for the future and in so doing, enable the facility to be more successful.

The management plan begins with the mission statement of the facility, its purpose, and its reason for being. If a board of directors were involved, this would be a good task for them to undertake. If not, the owners could make this determination. The Omnibus Budget Reconciliation Act (OBRA) in 1987, required nursing facilities to have a governing board that might establish general policies that would provide the general operating principles for the facility. The mission statement is the first step in this process. It should identify what the facility is attempting to accomplish. It answers the question "Why are we in existence?" In many ways it is a purpose statement. This statement serves as the corner stone of the management plan. It should be visible and shared with employees as they begin their employment and with residents when they move into the facility. The mission statement should be found on the collateral material provided by the marketing department and on the facility website. It says why the facility exists and can be a reminder to employees and residents alike.

The next step in the management plan is to put together a long rage plan. The plan should include goals to accomplish and direction for the growth or continued growth of the facility. Establishing goals, responsibilities and financial requirements will set the tone for the next five years. It is best to have three or four goals in the long rage plan. Be sure these goals are attainable and not simply a wish list. The goals should first of all relate to the mission statement. One goal may be to hire the best employees possible to provide care, food, socialization and services to the residents. The next question to answer is who is responsible for hiring these people? Usually it is the administrator or the department directors who do the hiring. The follow up questions are what will they do, when will they do it, where will they do it and how will they do it? By answering these questions, achieving the goal becomes someone's responsibility. After those questions are answered, the next question should be how much would it cost to accomplish this goal? If the goal were to hire the best employees, then one would assume there would be some advertising expenses, reference checks, criminal background checks, drug screenings and things of that nature. Recruiting is expensive. Determine how much it will cost to recruit, interview, and employee all the employees necessary to meet the mission statement. Also include money for at least a twenty-five percent turn over rate per year. When establishing the goals be sure to add the estimated costs involved in meeting the goals.

Below is an example of a Long Range Plan. Once a document such as this is completed with all the goals, it can be used as a blueprint of where the facility is going and how.

GOAL	OBJECTIVES Who, What, When, Were, How?	What will happen and where?	When?	Who is responsible?	How much?
1. Hire the best employees possible to provide care, food, socialization and services to the residents.	A. Ensure appropriately qualified staff are hired sufficient to meet resident needs	1. Expand classified advertising in newspapers and professional publications.	August 04	Administrator	$10,000
		2. Utilize behavioral interviewing guide	August 04	Department Directors	$0
		3. Encourage the continued use of annual evaluation guide	August 04	Administrator	$0
		4. Offer staff education to assure appropriate certification	September 04	Department Directors	$9,950
		5. Conduct an annual review of staffing levels	December 04	Administrator	$0

Once it is clear what the facility wants to do and how they plan to do it, the next step is to determine the organization and staffing required to accomplish these plans. If there is no organizational chart, prepare one showing who supervises whom and how the departments relate to one another. Use titles rather than employee names in the organizational chart. An example of an organizational chart is found in the previous chapter. This chart is also one that should be shared with new employees. It lets them know how they relate to whom within the organization. In most facilities, when the administrator is not in the building, the most senior nurse is in charge unless otherwise noted. Although the organizational chart does not show this, it is important that employees and residents know who is responsible when the administrator is not available. Some states require a written notice explaining who is responsible when the administrator is not present. Nurse supervisors are the normal answer on the evening and night shifts.

Look closely at each department to determine when staff members will be hired and how many will be needed. Hire only as needed and not before. Staffing is the most expensive cost to the long-term care facility. Employees will always say they need more help, so they cannot be the sole reason for hiring additional staff.

The following is an example of a chart that should be established to help set when new employees are hired based on occupancy.

# of Residents	# of Staff	Admin.	Marketing	Nursing	Dining	Housekeeping	Maintenance	Activities
1-10		1	1	7	1.5	1	1	1
10-20		1	1	11.2	2	1	1	1
20-30		1	1	15.4	3	1	1	1
30-40		1	1	19.6	4	1	1	1
40-50		2	1	23.8	5	1.5	1	1
50-60		2	1	28	6	1.5	1	1
60-70		2	2	32.2	6	1.5	1.5	1
70-80		2	2	36.4	6	1.5	1.5	1.5
80-90		2	2	40.6	7	1.5	1.5	1.5

Every facility is different, so these numbers will serve only as an example. If the community is a new one, it may make sense to put more money into a more marketing staff from the beginning to fill up the building faster. A small community may not be able to afford a receptionist, so the secretary may need to provide that function. A good, experienced director of nursing is the most important nursing position. Nursing facilities are required to have a director of nursing and unless it has fewer than 60 residents, to have another RN on duty at least eight hours per day. Assisted living facilities may not be required to have an RN, but it is a good suggestion. RN's come with more education and experience. In addition, having an RN makes the nursing care more creditable to physicians who treat residents there. After the director of nursing, it is important to have nursing staff supervisors on each shift. These should be RN's in a nursing home or LPN's, who can administer first aid, dispense medication, treat wounds, and supervise the work of others. In addition, certified nurse aides will be needed to assist residents with their activities of daily living. The number of aides needed will vary depending upon the amount of time that is required to effectively meet the needs of the residents. Dining staff can remain lower if the nurse aides are used to help serve meals. The activity staff my vary depending upon transportation needs. If the community provides transportation, then it may be necessary to add another activity person sooner. Look carefully at what services are being offered to the residents. Make sure that the staffing pattern is able to meet the needs of the residents according to what the contract has indicated will provided.

Create this management plan around full time equivalent (FTE) positions so that when it is time to prepare a budget, it is possible to go to this information as a first step. The plan can be adjusted as time goes by and should be reviewed annually for updates.

The chapter on human resources explains about the importance of job descriptions, but at this point it is important to say that the management plan should include an example of all the job descriptions and how many FTE's are needed at each job. This will make it easier to prepare an operating budget and to make sure all the goals, and needs are met during the planning stage.

The management plan should also include a description of each department and it's role in the operation of the facility. This is different than the job descriptions. This step indicates the purpose of each department, the services it provides and the number of employees who will work in each department. It explains what that department will accomplish and who will do it.

Here is an example.

Front Desk/ Receptionist
The front desk is the most visible part of the community to residents, staff and visitors. Those who staff the front desk have a wide range of responsibilities, which are directly, or indirectly, related to security, resident services, hospitality and marketing. The staff reports to the administrator.
Purpose:
To provide a welcoming center for visitors and guests.
To provide services to residents and staff.

To provide clerical/ secretarial support to the administrator.
To alert residents and staff to emergency situations.

Front Desk Services:
Greet residents and their guests, and provide assistance as appropriate.
Maintain visitor and volunteer sign in logs.
Maintain a "resident in" and "resident out" log
The desk will be staffed from 8:00 a.m. until 8:00 p.m. seven days a week.
Answer the telephone during Front Desk hours:
All department directors and nursing stations will have direct dial lines with voice mail; the switchboard will accept incoming calls on the general line, and all voice mail calls will be directed to the appropriate extension number.
Provide secretarial support to administrative staff and other departments as assigned.
Monitor the emergency alarms and calls received at the front desk and respond as necessary.
Take requests and arrange for:
Maintenance or housekeeping service
Provide general information to residents and the public.
This plan anticipates the involvement of the US Postal Service for the delivery of mail to resident mailboxes but the front desk personnel will distribute facility mail.
Assist residents with transportation needs:
Arrange for private transportation (taxi, limo, etc.)
Oversee the facility vehicle sign up book.
Assist residents with:
Dry cleaning pickup/delivery on a scheduled basis.
Receipt of deliveries (flowers, UPS, etc.)
Guest meal reservations.

Administrative Staff: Front Desk: FTE
Receptionist: 2.80

The next step in preparing a management plan is to prepare both a capital and an operating budget. These are prepared using the information found in the management plan thus far. For instance the administrator knows what they what to accomplish based on the mission statement that has been prepared. The goals indicate what the facility is trying to accomplish and how much it will cost to do so. The employee FTE's required to meet these goals and to operate the facility should also be included along with the cost of benefits, contracts and supplies need to operate a facility. There is more detail on budget preparation in the chapter on finance. The capital budget is also explained in greater detail in the chapter on finance but, simply put, the capital budget is prepared by anticipating what major capital expenditures the facility my incur in the next five years. These usually include equipment that costs more than $500.00 and will be used for more than a year. Items such as a new van or a new roof or a new stove and oven are the items found in a capital budget. It is important to include these two kinds of budgets in the management plan because they involve major expenditures and because they require thoughtful consideration and planning.

By working through the process of thinking about a mission statement, setting goals, developing staffing ratios for meeting those goals and budgets to provide appropriate income to support those goals, the management plan will serve as a master plan.

Chapter Six

Policies and Standards

Once the governing body or board of directors has established the mission or purpose for the long-term care facility, their next function is to create or approve policies. The purpose of these policies is to set standards by which the facility will be managed.

The regulations for nursing homes spell out this responsibility. Section 483.410 of the Code of Federal Regulations that deals with the responsibility of the governing body states, "The facility must have a governing body, or designated persons functioning as a governing body, that is legally responsible for establishing and implementing policies regarding the management and operation of the facility."[14]

Some of the other policies required by these same regulations are fundamental in the operation of a nursing facility. The first is one regarding advanced directives upon admission. It says, "The facility must comply with the requirements specified in subpart I of part 489 of this chapter relating to maintaining written policies and procedures regarding advance directives. These requirements include provisions to inform and provide written information to all adult residents concerning the right to accept or refuse medical or surgical treatment and, at the individual's option, formulate an advance directive."[15]

The second one is a policy that determines a readmission policy for residents who are hospitalized. The regulations say in section 483.12 of the Code of Federal Regulations, "Before a nursing facility transfers a resident to a hospital or allows a resident to go on therapeutic leave, the nursing facility must provide written information to the resident and a family member or legal representative that specifies

(i) The duration of the bed-hold policy under the State plan, if any, during which the resident is permitted to return and resume residence in the nursing facility; and

(ii) The nursing facility's policies regarding bed-hold periods, which must be consistent with paragraph (b)(3) of this section, permitting a resident to return."[16]

One final example of a reference to a required policy for nursing homes is regarding restraints. This policy is in Sec. 483.356 of the Code of Federal Regulations under "Protection of residents." The regulations states "(a) Restraint and seclusion policy for the protection of residents.

(1) Each resident has the right to be free from restraint or seclusion, of any form, used as a means of coercion, discipline, convenience, or retaliation.

(2) An order for restraint or seclusion must not be written as a standing order or on an as-needed basis.

(3) Restraint or seclusion must not result in harm or injury to the resident and must be used only

(i) To ensure the safety of the resident or others during an emergency safety situation; and

(ii) Until the emergency safety situation has ceased and the resident's safety and the safety of others can be ensured, even if the restraint or seclusion order has not expired.

(4) Restraint and seclusion must not be used simultaneously."[17]

After the overall governing policies are established, the next step is to have each department write policies and procedures that apply to how to perform functions within that department. The advantage of having policies and procedures is that everyone knows what is expected of them and there is no need to figure out how to do something over and over when a policy and procedure is in place to explain it. Once a policy and procedure is completed, it should be circulated to all who need to follow it and an in-service should be given to insure that all employees are aware of the new policy.

The following is an example of an outline for a policy and procedure.

Pleasant View Tong-term Care Facility Policy/Procedure

Title:
Initiating Department:
Primary Department Affected:
Associated Departments Affected:
Original Date of P/P:Revised date:

Policy:

Procedure:

The policy should state in broad strokes what will be done. The procedure should explain step by step what one should do.

Pleasant View long-term care Facility
Policy /Procedure

Title: Hiring of Staff

Initiating Department: Administration

Primary Department Affected: Administration

Associated Departments Affected: All Departments

Original Date of P/P:Revised date:

Policy:
When an opening occurs within a department, the department director will inform the administrator who will follow the steps in the accompanying procedure to secure a replacement if necessary.

Procedure:

When a new employee needs to be hired, the department director will submit a position requisition form to the administrator.

The administrator will advertise for the position if no appropriate applications are on file.

Once applications are received, the administrator will review them and submit the appropriate applicants to the department director for consideration.

The department directors will interview the applicants and perform reference checks on the applicant they feel best meets their needs and return all forms to administration.

The administrator will offer the position and set up drug screenings, TB tests and perform criminal background tests.

Once all tests are completed, the administrator will notify the Department Director and a beginning date will be agreed upon between the supervisor and the new employee.

Policies can be prepared for any routine or normal function. It is best if policies are discussed before they are enacted to insure that they accurately reflect what is expected. Once they are established, the staff should be held to them in insure consistency of procedures.

If there are State imposed standards or regulations that govern how the long-term care facilities should perform, they should be used to create a list of needed policies. The procedure portion may be spelled out in the regulations, but often times they are not, so establishing a procedure that makes sense for the operations within your building is essential.

In Virginia, one of the first standards for assisted living facilities talks about employee records and health requirements. It says:

"A record shall be established for each staff member. It shall not be destroyed until two years after employment is terminated.

Personal and social data to be maintained on employees are as follows:
Name
Birth date
Current address and telephone number
Position and date employed
Last previous employment
Two reference checks reflecting the date of the reference, the source and the content

An original criminal record report and sworn disclosure statement
Previous experience or training or both
Social security number
Name and telephone number of person to contact in an emergency
Notations of formal training received following employment
Date and reason for termination of employment

By reviewing this regulation, it is obvious that a number of policies could be generated to ensure that this standard is met. The first one is that a record shall be established for each employee. We normally call this an employee file or a human resource file. In that file should be all the information required. The application for employment should include the name, address and phone number, last previous employment, previous experience, social security number and emergency contact. Additional forms should be used for reference checks, criminal records reports, formal training following employment and date and reason for termination. The second policy could be about how to make reference checks including a procedure on placing the completed forms in the HR file The third could be on obtaining a criminal reference check with procedures regarding payment for the check and placement in the HR file. The fourth policy could be about termination procedures including the need to complete appropriate forms and include them in the HR file. The last policy related to this standard is regarding how long employee records will be stored. It could include a procedure regarding removing the file from the active employee file drawer and storing it in an appropriate place.

It is easy to see how policies can be written about nearly all the standards or regulations we adhere to in the assisted living industry. Access to these policies should be easy so that new employees can read them and quickly learn how the facility wants things done.

Occasionally, as a means of assuring quality, and of meeting the standards, the next step is to prepare checklists. They do not apply to everything, but a checklist for this standard could be located on the inside of the file folder and used to make sure all appropriate material according to the policy is completed. The following is an example.

Employee File Checklist
Employee name:_____
_____Application
_____Two reference checks
_____Criminal record report
_____Formal training, post hire
Date of training: Topic:

_____Termination date

The checklist included in the chapter on housekeeping is another example of how a checklist can be used. A policy on cleaning a resident room could be prepared with the checklist to follow.

The next step is to develop standards of operations. Not all things require a policy, but having a standard for everyone to work toward can help insure that the same service will be provided to the residents no matter who is performing the task.

Dignity

Standard:
Each resident shall receive care in a manner and in an environment that maintains or enhances each resident's dignity and respect in full recognition of his or her individuality.
Procedures:
Interaction between facility staff and residents will show that each resident's self worth is maintained or enhanced, as evidenced by the following:
1. Activity staff/volunteers will interact with residents and carry out activities, which assist the resident to maintain and enhance his/her self-worth.
2. Personal grooming activity classes will be offered and adapted for residents with cognitive impairments.

3. Residents will be dressed cleanly and appropriately for the time of day, season, and individual preference when participating in facility activities— indoors and/or outdoors.

4. Activity staff/volunteers will afford residents as much privacy as is practicable during activities requiring personal assistance to the resident.

5. Residents' private space and property will be respected. Staff/ volunteers will not disturb or use resident personal belongings in any way without the resident's permission.

6. The actions and intentions of staff will be communicated to the resident prior to provision of care, transport, or beginning of an activity.

7. Residents will be addressed by a name of the resident's choice. Staff will speak courteously, listen carefully, and treat residents with respect. Residents will not be addressed as Honey, Dearie, Grandma, etc., unless per resident request.

8. Staff/volunteers will knock on resident door and wait for affirmative response prior to entering resident's room.

9. Resident preferences shall be considered in all aspects of the resident's daily life including activity participation, daily schedules, and routines.

10. Staff/volunteers shall communicate directly with resident and not around resident, regardless of cognitive abilities.

11. Activities director will report any concerns regarding facility/resident dignity issues to the administrator.

Here is another one for activities that shows a standard and gives procedures or steps to take to meet the standard.

Equipment Maintenance
Standard:
All mechanical, electrical and other activity appliances, equipment and supplies shall be maintained in sanitary, safe, operating condition.
Procedures:

1. All appliances, equipment, and supplies will be examined prior to each use or on a monthly/quarterly basis, whichever is most appropriate. All defective items are repaired or replaced to ensure that standard for safety and cleanliness are met.

2. Appliances, equipment and/or supplies requiring maintenance will not be used until safety standards have been met/restored. Such items will be

labeled unsafe for use by attaching a red tag or lockout box to the cord or plug, and removing from area when possible, to prevent accidental use. Items unable to be safely repaired shall be replaced.

3. A monthly maintenance and cleaning schedule checklist shall be established and maintained for all activity appliances, equipment, and supplies.

A. The activity director will establish frequency maintenance checks and cleaning schedule for all appropriate activity appliances, equipment, and supplies.

B. Dates and initials of individual(s) completion maintenance check or cleaning will be document each applicable month.

4.The activity staff, volunteers, and residents will be oriented to safety procedures and proper use of activity equipment prior to independent use by the individual(s).

A.The activity staff's orientation and training regarding equipment will be documented on the individual's orientation form within the first month of employment. Orientation to additional equipment will be documented on the maintenance and cleaning checklist with staff's signature and date.

B. Volunteer and resident orientation/training will be documented on the maintenance and cleaning checklist with individual's signature and date.

5. Equipment and supplies will be cleaned with appropriate disinfectant(s) as determined and approved by facility's housekeeping personnel.

6. Equipment and supplies used for residents in isolation will be maintained and cleaned in accordance with facility infection control policies and procedures.

7. The equipment maintenance and cleaning checklist will be kept on file for a minimum of one year.

These standards are examples. Each department can set standards based on regulations or expectations and share them with their staff.

The Department Directors can in-service their staff using these standards and hold their staff accountable for meeting the standards in their daily work.

This standard is an example of one to be used in the nursing department. The standards can take various shapes, but the important thing is that the standard spells out what steps are to be taken each time a function occurs.

Compress Application, Cool (Moist)

STANDARD OPERATING PROCEDURE
Resident Care, III
Department, Category Risk, Time Required

Description: To relieve inflammation and swelling, to reduce body temperature

Equipment, Supplies, Materials
Compress material   *   Thermometer
Prescribed solution *   Container with ice
Emesis basin   *   Plastic sheeting
Towel
==
Procedure
Steps   Explanation/Key Points

The following procedure is to be performed only by **Licensed Personnel**.

1. Explain procedure to Health Center Resident and recognize Health Center Resident's right to refuse treatment. If Health Center Resident refuses treatment, counsel regarding alternatives, document and notify physician.

2. Provide full visual privacy and to the extent possible auditory privacy.

3. Bring equipment or necessary items to bedside. Wash hands thoroughly.

Steps

4. Take resident's temperature before beginning cold application.
Compress Application, Cool (Moist)

Explanation/Key Points

5. Place plastic sheeting and towel beneath the area to be treated.

Avoid unnecessary exposure

6. Position Resident so they are comfortable and supported—recumbent or in chair with table for support.

7. Moisten compress material with cool solution.

Apply compress to site.
Compresses are usually ordered for 15-20 minutes.

8. Check vital signs during treatment and stop treatment immediately if signs of irregularity occur.

9. Check resident's skin beneath the cool application for blanching or cyanosis at frequent intervals. If it occurs, discontinue treatment immediately.

10. Remove cool compresses and discard all disposables in plastic bag. Wash hands thoroughly.

11. Take temperature on completion of treatment.

12. Leave resident dry and comfortable.

13. Remove reusable items for cleaning.

14. Document interventions, observations and outcomes as it relates to this procedure.

One word of warning regarding setting policies and standards; they can be very helpful for staff but if they are not followed and a resident is hurt or killed, the prosecuting attorney could use the standards and policies to hold the facility accountable. Standards that go beyond the federal or state regulations are the ones that the attorney will be able to use to hold the facility accountable above and beyond what the law requires.

By providing standards, in-servicing employees on these standards and holding them accountable for working within the standards, the long-term care facility will be assured consistency of care and practice.

Chapter Seven

Communication

A leader must be a good communicator. Communication is both passing along information and receiving it. Before the administrator of a facility can pass along information to the staff, he/she must understand it. We receive information by listening, reading and observing. All of what we receive is filtered by our own background, needs, interpretation and agendas. It is possible to have two people hear the same information and respond to it differently. The administrator must be aware of his/her own filters and be aware that when he/she is passing along information, it will also be filtered by those receiving it.

There are many different types of personality tests available that point out differences in people. The Myers-Briggs type indicator is one that is based on the earlier work of Carl Jung. This instrument indicates a wide variety of things about us, but as a tool for helping us be better communicators, it is important to know these basic personality types. According to this tool, there are four areas that show opposite styles. The first comparison is between extroverts and introverts. The extrovert will process information externally. They enjoy being with other people, are happy in large groups and are eager to talk. The introvert, on the other hand, processes information internally. They like to be by themselves, prefer to work in small groups, and appear reluctant to share their thoughts. The second comparison is between intuitive and sensing. Someone who is sensing seems to be interested in the details, what can be learned from seeing, tasting, hearing, feeling and smelling. They enjoy the process of getting from step one to step ten even more than the result. The sensing person will follow the plan and enjoy the procedure, but may not be very good at making the plan in the first place. On the other hand, the intuitive person is one who sees the big picture and can envision goals and missions. They love to be the starters and leave the implementation up to the sensing people. The third comparison is between feeling and thinking.

Feeling people are interested in relationships, values and fairness. They often decide things on a feeling. Thinking people, on the other hand are much more analytical. They are interested in knowing the rules and following them. The final comparison is between perceiving and judging personalities. The perceiving person gets together data from a variety of sources, processes it and finally decides. The judging person wants to make quick decisions, is interested in getting it done and moving on. They tend to work best with a list they can check off and enjoy order rather than confusion.

The indicator normally is able to tell you if you are either an extrovert or an introvert, a person who is more comfortable using his senses to gather information or is more intuitive, a feeling person or one who is analytical, a thinking person, and finally, a perceiving person when it comes to decision making or a judging person. Knowing where you fit into these four categories will help you understand how you receive information. If you tend to be extroverted, you will want to talk about what has been shared with you. Chances are you will ask questions of clarifications or even share a story of an event in your own life that was similar to what had just been told you. If you are introverted, you may receive information, say thank you and go on with your day processing internally what was said, why it was said, how it was said and what it might mean. If you are a sensing person you may hear something and want to know more about the information, how it was attained, how accurate it was and how to move on from what had been communicated. The intuitive person may hear the same information and begin to see plans for getting started with a solution. The feeling person may be concerned about how what has been communicated might seem fair or unfair to themselves or others hearing the same information. They may not like what they are hearing, but for the sake of a good relationship accept it. The thinking person may hear something and begin to set parameters of what would be an acceptable response. The perceiving person may be able to receive information from one source and listen to comments from a variety of others before coming up with a comment that pulls discussion together and enables a group to move onto the next step. Finally, the judging person may hear something and instantly decide if they accept it or not or what their response needs to be.

Knowing a little about the staff will also help the administrator know how they will receive information and how they will present it. The extroverts will approach you to say hello while the introverts will not. The extroverts will be seen talking in the hallways and offices in small groups. They will dominate the conversation at the lunch table and entertain residents with a joke or a quick story. The introvert will stay to him or herself and keep their thoughts to themselves. The intuitive person is great in planning and goal setting, but the sensing person will fill in the blanks and develop step-by-step procedures to achieve the goals. The thinking person will want to see the employee handbook and the policies and procedures to make sure that he is doing his job just the way it should be done. The feeling person will be the advocate for the person who runs out of sick days and tries to get you to change the policies or ignore them for the sake of the sick co-worker. The perceiving person is great to have when trying to decide what to do in a group setting. They will listen and then come up with an answer that seems quite acceptable to all. The judging person is not so interested in hearing all sides and exploring all options when a decision is to be made. If someone called out sick more than the allotted times, the decision is easy, they are fired.

Listening is a major part of communication. But as has been explained above, we are all different and receive and pass along information differently. In addition, we all come with our histories, or filters, that determine how we hear what we hear. We may listen less intently to a subordinate and more intently to a supervisor. The same may be true to our listening to a man as apposed to a woman or a young person as opposed to an older person.

Sydney Finkelstein was quoted earlier in the chapter on administration. He encourages openness in companies as a means of helping the leaders correct mistakes or make decisions. He says "The name of the game is to make it as easy as possible for people to count, to be heard, to have a voice; while a culture of open-mindedness is a critical prerequisite, it's important to back it up with multiple avenues of debate, discussion and data."[18]

Listening to suggestions, complaints and concerns can help the administrator do his/her job better. Making it possible for employees to make suggestions, to complain and to share concerns is the first step in developing a culture of open-mindedness. It is essential that the administrator listen to the employees. Take what they say and compare it with the other information available before making any changes in policy or direction. Again, Finkelstein says, "People have to believe that their contributions matter that no one will shoot the messenger. They have to trust that honesty, good intentions, and well-thought-out decisions will be valued and respected."[19] Listening, being open to suggestions, acting or explaining decisions all help to establish open dialogue and create a more positive work environment.
Levels of Communication

Communication has within it several levels. It is important to understand them as we struggle to deal with others. Many times residents, families and staff will come to the administrator because they are upset about something. It is important that the administrator be able to listen without being defensive if the issue brought up is to be solved and emotions brought under control. It is best to listen, to pay attention, to take notes and to clarify any misunderstanding before proceeding to any other steps. Ask questions of the person who has come to you to get as much information as possible. Ask for the facts, as they know them. If they are recounting an event, ask them to describe what literally occurred, not what they thought or felt, but only what literally occurred. By doing this, you avoid having to sort through the feelings and emotions to get to the facts. It is best if you can take notes as they are telling you what has made them so upset. Once they have shared the facts with you, spend time reviewing these facts to be sure you have them in the correct sequence. Ask questions of clarification during this review to be sure that you understand the details of what has gotten the other person upset to the point of coming in to talk to you. Understand that getting the facts from one person is like asking five people who are blindfolded to describe an elephant. The person who feels and smells a leg will describe the leg. The person who feels and smells the tail will describe a tail. Likewise, the people feeling the trunk and ears will describe what they believe to be the facts. It is important to hear from as many people as possible about an incident before making a decision as to what actually happened and how to deal with it.

On a second level, people who come to the administrator will be expressing not simply the facts, which is what is essential for understanding a problem, but also opinions. Opinions are offered after someone has reviewed the facts. They see or hear something and come to a conclusion, which is an opinion. For instance the person talking to you may say that a fellow employee was late again today. That is a fact. Then they may add, "you need to put her on a suspension", which is their opinion of what should be done. Try to separate facts from opinions by once again asking clarifying questions. Determine what actually happened, how it happened and why it happened. Once the facts are ascertained, it is possible to deal with the opinions expressed. The administrator may say, "Let me check into this and then I would like to talk with you more about why you think your coworker should be suspended." Or a simple "thank you for your opinion" would carry the same message. A third level of communication is feeling or emotions. Oftentimes conversations can be emotional. People may express anger or sadness as they communicate with you. Once the facts and opinions are weeded out, it is important to understand that emotions may be the driving force for the conversation in the first place. Sentences that begin with "I feel…" are expressions of emotion. The person you are talking to may say, "I feel angry that you have lost my mothers ring. You should find the thief and fire them." Of course, you did not lose it. The fact is it is lost. The opinion is that it was the facilities responsibility and the emotion made it personal. You lost it. The steps discussed above will help clarify what actually happened. Weed out the facts. Is the ring missing? Who discovered it missing? Deal with the opinion about firing the thief by assuring the person reporting the missing object that if it is determined that one of the employees actually took the ring, you would follow the facility disciplinary policy.

And finally, on the third level, deal with the emotion expressed. In this case the person is angry and you are the one getting the blast. Try to not respond in anger or defense. Let the other person express him or herself. When they are through, deal with the emotion. Something like, "I understand that you are upset about the loss of this ring," will enable the person to talk some more about their feelings. It is better to have them sharing with the administrator than other family members or oversight agencies. Everybody feels better if someone else listens to him or her express their emotion. But it essential that once the emotion is expressed, there is some sort of agreement on what will be done. The best thing to do is to promise a speedy investigation and a call to them as soon as possible to let them know what decision has been made to deal with the problem. Communication is a little like getting to know someone on a first date. Facts are shared easily, like what someone likes or where they have lived, or perhaps, their occupation. At some point, conversations may go a step deeper and involve an opinion about a city or a sports team or a profession. As people become comfortable with one another, they may share an emotion, a fear, anger, and a joy. Emotions like fear or joy are normally shared after people feel comfortable talking with each other. Responding to an emotion with words that tell the other person you understand them and are concerned for them will enable them to share more of the same. To insure that residents, families and staff will feel comfortable sharing with you requires that the administrator spend time talking to these people before an event occurs that brings them to the administrator or to the agency that supervises the facility.

Verbal, Nonverbal and Written Communication

We communicate to many forms. The three most obvious are the verbal, the nonverbal and the written. The verbal type of communication is what we say. This seems pretty straightforward. But, there are many ways to say things that create different meanings. If someone says, "Where did you get that outfit?" the meaning of the question may depend the tone used to ask the question. It could be a compliment if the voice is higher and full of enthusiasm. Or it could be a snide remark if asked with a bit of a sneer. Or it could simply be a direct question. How we say what we say determines what others interpret our meaning to be. Sarcasm is a way of saying something using words that may appear to be positive but saying them in such a way as to imply just the opposite. Verbal communication can be misleading and not so direct.

Nonverbal communication is simply communicating without saying anything. The classic example of non-verbal communication is crossed arms or legs. These normally imply that the person is not receptive to listening to what you have to say. Open arms and leaning toward the speaker implies that there is interest in what is being said. Making a statement followed by touching ones nose normally implies that the person is not telling the truth. A look between friends can communicate, "Did you hear that?" or "I told you she would say that." A raised eyebrow could imply some doubt. A frown expresses disappointment or disapproval. Raising your eyes may indicate that you are thinking about something. A furrowed brow may indicate that one is thinking about what was just said. Smiles normally imply that everything is fine.

Written communication is perhaps the most direct because it requires that you say what you mean. E-mails these days are often quick responses that get right to the point. Letters tend to require more thought and normally require better grammar.

Understanding that people will communicate in various ways and send and receive information in various ways will help with misunderstandings in the future. It is always best if you are not sure what is being said to simply ask directly for clarification rather than assume you understand if there is any doubt.

As a long-term care administrator, it is important to understand that communication with an older person carries with it some extra obstacles. Some degree of impaired vision and hearing is common with most people who live in a long-term care facility. When speaking to one of these older people, try doing some of the following:

Stand in front of the person and if possible, at their eye level, so they are aware that you are there and can focus their attention upon you.

Gently touch the older person to get their attention before you begin to speak.

Call the older person by name before you begin to speak.

If the person is hearing impaired, make sure they can see your face and especially your mouth as you speak.

Speak slowly and clearly.

Many hearting impaired people are able to hear lower tones easier than higher tones. Try to use a lower voice when speaking to them.

Use gestures to help demonstrate your point.

Give the older person time to respond before moving on to the next question.

If an important conversation is planned with a resident who is hearing impaired, take them to a quiet area so that background noise does not interfere with the conversation.

Be sure that assistive devices are in use before deigning a conversation. Hearing aides, and glasses, if worn as assistive devices, should be made available to the resident each morning. It is best if the nurse checks to make sure the batteries are working as the resident gets prepared for the day. If hearing aides are not available, provide a pen and pad to allow the resident to communicate their needs.

Being a good communicator is essential if one is to be a good administrator. Listening carefully to what others are saying is the first step in communication. There are people who are comfortable speaking their think. These are the people who dominate group discussions and conversations. They may, after hearing someone else share their view, change what they think and begin to say something different. Their opinion seems to change and they are easily swayed. There are others who think their speak. They are not the first ones to offer an opinion. They often sit back and listen to opposing views and finally say something quite profound. Their opinions are often the ones others agree with when the discussion is concluded. Listening carefully to what others think and say will enable the administrator to hear other opinions and make a well-informed decision.

Chapter Eight

Customer Service

Long-term care facilities, because of their nature and the competition they face, must be concerned about customer service. Simply put, customer service is improving how the facility deals with its customers. This is not just a function of marketing or administration, but if it is done well, providing good customer service will enhance marketing and cut down on the number of complaints to which the administrator must respond.

The following is an example of good customer service. A man went to a store and bought a suit for a convention wherein he was to be a speaker the following week. He selected a suit and was told to come back in six days so that the appropriate alterations could be made to the suit. The day before the convention, the man came back to the store to pick up the suit. When he got there, he was told that the suit was not done yet. Upset, the customer asked what he was supposed to do. The clerk told him to go to the convention and that he would have the suite sent there overnight. The customer left the store and packed an old suite just in case the new one did not arrive. Shortly after the man checked into his hotel, the front desk called to tell him a package had arrived for him. He got the package and noticed that it was from the store where he had purchased the new suit. He was pleasantly surprised. He took the package to his room and opened it. Inside was the suite he had purchased and an extra sports coat with a note that read, "Sorry for the delay, we hope you will enjoy the sports coat with our compliments." Now, the question is, where do you think the man went to buy his next suit?

Not everything goes as planned. The questions that we face when things go poorly are "How are we going to respond to this? How can we make lemon-aide out of these lemons? What can we do to make this situation better?" The answers to these questions are not always easy to obtain, but the golden rule is always a good place to start. By asking, "How would I like to be treated if I were the other person?" or "What would serve to calm me down?" one can begin the process of providing good customer service.

Thinking these situations through may provide the answers needed to turn a bad situation into a good one.

As we consider how best to provide good customer service, it is important to be able to identify who the customer is in a long-term care facility. Perhaps you could begin by asking, "Who do we serve?" The answers will vary, but they should include:
residents
potential residents
families
physicians
clergy
visitors
outside contractors
volunteers
guests
delivery personnel

The next question to ask is "What do we do for them?"
residents: meals, cleaning, maintenance, nursing care, security…
potential residents: information, tours, meals, invitations
families: peace of mind, information, meals
physicians: provide care to their patients, information, feedback, assistance
clergy: information, meals, opportunities to visit their members
visitors: information, a safe place, hospitality, meals
outside contractors: employment opportunities, business example
volunteers: a place to serve, meals, training
guests: meals, security, a place to visit friends
delivery personnel: a safe, comfortable environment.

"When do we provide this service?" is the next question.
residents: some of these service are provided 24 hours per day, others will be provided as needed.
potential residents: when they visit or when we send them information
families: they will have peace of mind 24 hours per day. Information will be provided via a newsletter or in family meetings. Meals will be made available upon request and at the monthly family night dinner.
physicians: care will be provided to their patients 24 hours a day. Feedback will be given to them concerning their patient as requested.

The third question regarding customers is "Where do we provide this service?"

residents: care will be given within the facility, as we transport to the physicians or while out of the facility participating in an activity.

potential residents: information will be provided in the facility, in their homes and via our website. Tours will be given in the facility.

Families: information will be provided via our newsletter. Meals will be provided at the facility and lodging in our guest room.

The final question to be asked about these customers is "How do we provide this service?"

residents: services will be provide by our staff through schedules and communication methods established to meet the resident's needs.

potential residents: information and tours will be provided by the marketing personnel and the administrator. Meals will be provided by the dining service staff after marketing makes the appropriate arrangements.

Going through this exercise of determining who the customers are, what we do for them, and when, where, and how we provide it, will serve to help the entire staff better understand that their job is not limited to what is found in the job description. Good customer service is everyone's job.

Providing good customer service requires at a minimum, meeting our contractual agreements. Once it has been determined who customers are, it is important to try to determine what these customers expect from the facility. Although we try to spell out the services we will provide in a contract with our residents, they always come with expectations that have not been discussed nor are they listed in the contract. One example of such an expectation is scheduled transportation. To some that might mean that the facility will take the resident anywhere so long as the resident schedules the trip. To others, the expectation may mean that friends may be picked up at their homes to participate in scheduled transportation. Still others may think that the driver will wait for them while they go shopping or see the doctor. From this simple example it is easy to see that residents can and do interpret what the facility says it will do in a variety of ways. It is impossible to define every service in a contract, but it is also important to try to make clear what the facility will do for the residents prior to their move in.

It would be a good exercise to have each department director list what their department provides the residents and then to compare it to what is written in the contract about what will be provided. It is absolutely essential that everything promised in the contract be provided. Where the problems arise, as sighted in the example above, is the interpretation of what the residents think the words mean as opposed to what administration thinks the words mean.

The second level of customer service is trying to determine what is not in the contracts but is simply assumed by the residents. Food seems to be the biggest area were assumptions are different than what is provided. Most people who become residents in long-term care facilities have been cooking food the way they like it for fifty years. They assume the grilled cheese sandwich the cook prepares will taste the same as the ones they have made, with the same kind of cheese and browned to the same color. They assume the tomato soup will be made mixed with water or perhaps mixed with milk just as they had made it over the years. They assume the eggs, oatmeal, pancakes, sausage, juice and coffee will be done the same way, look the same and taste the same as they have had it for fifty years. The same assumptions are made in every level of service provided by the facility. Is the underwear folded or not? Are the pullover shirts folded or hung? Is the toilet paper soft enough? Is the call bell answered within thirty seconds? Are the kick-knacks dusted each week? Are the furnace filters changed monthly? Is the music in the lobby too loud or too soft? The residents come with unspoken expectations. Their happiness is usually based on how well the facility has met these unspoken expectations.

The task of the staff is to try to find out what these unspoken expectations are. Once they are known, then it can be determined if the facility can meet them or not. One way to determine these unspoken expectations is to ask about them. If the department directors visit the new residents and ask questions about how their department has met or not met needs and expectations, a list can be prepared and the issued discussed with the administrator. A second way is a survey that allows residents to make comments after each question. A third method of gathering information is a residents council meeting or a family meeting that is designed to discuss expectations. It takes effort and patience and inquiries to iron out the differences between what residents expect and what the facility provides.

The role of the facility is to meet the contractual agreement and the standards set forth by governing agencies. It is also desirable to try to understand the unspoken expectations and to try to meet as many of these as possible.

Once the administrator knows the unspoken expectations, the next step is to determine how to meet these expectations. Some may be easy while others may be impossible. Prepare the list and review it. Determine what can be done without adding additional expense. Next determine what can be done and how much it will cost to do these things. By charging for services beyond the scope of the contract, residents may be happier and the services will not affect the budget. A good example of this may be additional housekeeping or additional care required. By charging for the service, the resident gets their needs met and the facility is compensated for it.

The last step in providing good customer service is to go beyond what is agreed upon and beyond what is expected in an attempt to exceed expectations. In the story of the man and his suit, the store met its obligation to have the suit the man paid for to him in time for the convention. But it went beyond that obligation by giving the man a sports coat as well. Although in the long-term care industry we do not often have repeat customers, word of mouth from residents to their friends and from their families to their friends is a powerful marketing tool. It may cost something to please people when a mistake has been made or obligation not met, but unless some overture is made to please the customer, negative comments will be shared with potential residents.

Once again, ask the department directors how they think the facility might exceed the expectations they have heard voiced by the residents or their families. Look at this list and determine what is possible. Determine in each given situation the negative affect of not going above and beyond.

Good customer service can begin by asking "What else can I do for you?" or by saying "I'm sorry we made that mistake." By asking how else we might be of service, we are telling the customer that we are willing to do more or to go farther or to go the extra mile. By saying we are sorry about a mistake and assuring the person that we will do all in our power to correct it, only puts us back even. This is what is expected. Flowers, candy, free cable for a week, or a free sports coat helps us exceed the expectations.

All that we have said about our residents in the preceding paragraphs applies also to the rest of our customers. Obviously the facility must meet the contractual obligation of any customer, but they must also strive to exceed those obligations for each of their customers. Accomplishing this task will result in happy residents, happy families, happy staff members and hopefully, a successful business.

Chapter Nine

Continuous Quality Improvement

Continuous Quality Improvement is a data driven process for improving performance. It is fueled by discussions and evaluations for necessary change that uses measurement and analysis techniques to prevent problems or uncover opportunities for making positive change.

CQI is a philosophy based on the belief that we can always do better and that each time we find a mistake or error or omission, it is an opportunity to improve. Adopting this philosophy allows people to find a chance to make the business better before the customer is affected adversely.

CQI is a method of administration that is designed to be a system of performance monitoring. Monitors can be set up for each department and for areas within each department. The easiest way to establish these monitors is to read through the state regulations that govern the way long-term care Living Facilities do business. Indicate what the standard is for each item, and then ask in the survey if the standard has been meet or not. If not, then a committee or a department would try to brainstorm about how to make the changes necessary to enable the facility to comply with the standard.

Below is a typical monitor based upon a state regulation regarding staff training and orientation.

Standard	Met	How met	Not Met	Corrective action proposed
Employees made aware of the purpose of the facility?				
Employees made aware of the service provided?				
Employees made aware of the daily routines?				
Employees made aware of required regulations as it relates to their duties?				
Employees aware of facility disaster plans?				
Employees aware of the use of a first aid kit and its location?				
Employees aware of the procedures for detecting and reporting suspected abuse, neglect or exploitation?				
Employees aware of techniques for assisting residents in overcoming transfer trauma?				
Employees aware of Fire drill procedures?				

These standards can be met through an orientation process. Once someone has completed orientation, it is possible to sign off saying that the employee is aware. The standard has been met. The answer to how the standard was met in this case was during orientation. In other cases it may be in-service training or training outside the facility. If the standard has not been met, then there is a space to indicate how it could be met.

The Health Department probably will inspect the facility kitchen for cleanliness, food temperatures, food storage, food handling etc. Using the inspector's form, it is possible to put together a standard that the dietary department is expected to meet. Here is an example.

Standard	Met	How Met	Not met	Corrective Action Proposed
Food temperature in dining room 160-170				
Portion Size:				
Soup 4 to 8 oz.				
Entrée' 3 oz.				
Starch ½ cup				
Vegetable ½ cup				
Hot Beverage 8oz.				
Salad ½ cup				
Dessert ½ cup				
Fruit ½ cup				
Cold beverage 8oz.				
Equipment Temp. checklist:				
Freezer: below 0 degrees				
Cooler: below 40 degrees				
Milk machine: below 40 degrees				
Dishwasher:				
Wash temp: 160				
Rinse temp. 180				

There could be a logbook put together with this kind of checklist in it. These check lists are called quality indicators. Each day someone should go through the list. If the items did not measure up to what was expected, it would be noted and a process would begin to make the necessary corrections. Once the corrections were put into place, the items would continue to be monitored. If there is any deviation, once again it is noted and once again a process would be put into place to make the necessary corrections.

The Quality Improvement Cycle follows these steps:
1. A problem is identified.
2. A solution is suggested.
3. The solution is tested.
4. If the problem is not corrected, the process begins again at #1.

The quality improvement process begins with identifying a project. The questions to ask at this point are:

"Is this a chronic problem?"
"Is it important?"
"Is it of manageable size?"
"Is it able to be measured?"

The next questions asked are related to determine if indeed the problem is related to quality improvement.

"Are you trying to reach a new level of performance?" (Are you trying to do something better?)

"Do you have measurable specific deficiencies or opportunities for performance improvements?"

"Are you trying to find and eliminate the root cause of a problem?"

The next step is to establish the project. After looking at options, determine that this particular project is the one you want to undertake. Once that is done establish a mission statement that is specific, measurable, observable and manageable. Then select a team to work on the project. This team should be made up of those most closely associated with the project.

The third step is to diagnose the cause of the problem identified. To do this one must analyze the symptoms, formulate theories, test them and finally identify the root cause. Testing the theory entails putting some sort of test together that will enable you to gather appropriate measurable information. Once it is collected, it needs to be analyzed to determine if your original theory was correct or if the data suggests another cause for the problem at hand.

Step four is the opportunity to remedy the problem. At this stage one would evaluate the alternatives, design a remedy, design controls and implement. Quality controls include things like the means to measure the results of the new process, determining how actual performance will be measured against the standard, designing action steps to regulate performance if it does not meet the standard and establishing self-control for the staff members involved.

There should be a Quality Improvement team in place to establish the standards for each department, to get reports on the results of the monitors that have been put in place, and to make recommendations on how to improve in a particular area. It works best to have the department directors serve as the Quality Improvement team until others begin to understand how the process works, and then others can take their place if necessary.

Many communities add to Quality Improvement a program on continual assessment or quality assessment. The Quality Assessment and Improvement

Committee (QA&I) then together provide a mechanism for Continuous Quality Improvement (CQI) for facility operations.

Process:

Activities to continuously monitor and evaluate the quality and appropriateness of services provided should be carried out according to the attached Quality Assessment and Improvement Plan.

QA&I Activities should be designed and used to:

Identify problems or areas in need of attention, and/or

Measure outcomes of care or services provided

Identify opportunities of improving the care or services provided.

Someone should be appointed to serve as QA&I Coordinator by the Quality Assessment and Improvement Committee. They should be responsible for coordinating all activities listed in the Quality Assessment and Improvement Plan.

Information generated through QA&QI activities should be used to promote the continuous improvement in both the quality and appropriateness of resident care services.

Customer satisfaction with the level of services provided should be an integral component of the Quality Assessment and Improvement plan.

A formal QI report should be prepared and presented to the Facility Quality Assessment and Improvement Committee on a quarterly basis with a yearly summary.

Using this kind of assessment and improvement program will help an administrator identify problems, note trends, and make appropriate corrections in a timely manner.

Most nursing homes have a Quality Assessment and Assurance program to enable them to note problem areas and make appropriate changes as quickly as possible. These are usually interdisciplinary meetings including the medical director, the administrator, The director of nursing, the pharmacist, the therapists, the dietitian, and the department directors. Reporting on findings from the quality indicators and discussing a plan of correction for areas that are of concern enable the whole team to be involved in making corrections. This committee meets at least quarterly to hear the reports of the departments using their quality indicators. If necessary plans of action are developed there so that the necessary improvements can be made.

There has been a lot of discussion regarding how to protect this self-assessment information from inspectors as they come in for their annual review. The Code of Federal Regulations states in section 483.75 that "A

State or the Secretary may not require disclosure of the records of such committee except in so far as such disclosure is related to the compliance of such committee with the requirements of this section.

(4) Good faith attempts by the committee to identify and correct quality deficiencies will not be used as a basis for sanctions."[20]

Part Three
Department Overview

Chapter Ten

Activities

This third section to the book deals with the many different departments that are involved in a long-term care facility. This chapter deals with activities. Following it are dining, finance, housekeeping, human resources, maintenance, marketing, and nursing. By reading these chapters, one will get a clear understanding of how all are essential to the service provided to residents in long-term care settings.

Activities can play an important role in the resident's physical and emotional well-being. An activity program that includes physical movement, intellectual stimulation, religious services and entertainment will keep the resident physically and mentally alert. It is important that the person who leads this department understands the limitations of the elderly so that physical exercises chosen are appropriate. It is just as important that they also understand that the elderly may be frail physically, but they are not children. Crafts should be appropriate and not child like. Exercise and stimulation can assist residents as they transition from their homes to the long-term care facility. Planning activities that are varied and that consider the abilities, physical conditions, needs and interests of the residents will ensure that residents are happy and their needs are met.

The place to begin planning is by taking the time to talk to the residents, reviewing their assessments and social histories and listening to families as they share what their parents or loved ones enjoyed before coming to the long-term care facility. Once some information is gathered, begin to work with a calendar on which to write out the month's schedule of activities. By looking at the whole month, the Activity Director can see if the activities meet the standards of diversity including activities that are physical, interactive, social, religious and entertaining. Once it is complete, it should be posted before the month begins and kept for at least three months. Posting the calendar enables everyone to see it and plan his or her month around the activities. Keeping a copy of the calendar helps the planner and also answers questions state regulators might have about the number of activities offered to residents.

All residents should be encouraged to participate, but not required. For nursing home residents, the activity may require a staff member to come to them in their rooms where reading or card games may occur. Any restrictions imposed by a physician must be documented and honored.

Exercise is important for people of any age, but the right exercise is especially important for the elderly. The elderly, even those who are wheelchair bound, can do a chair exercise following the instructions of a leader or even those on videotape. If videotape is used, an activity aide should be present to assist and encourage. Programs designed for the elderly, such as *Body Recall* help to keep all parts of the body limber. They encourage the elderly to use their fingers and toes, their hands and feet, their legs and arms. A variety of physical exercises are important to keep interest and to keep the bodies moving.

It is important to provide equipment for exercise that the residents will feel comfortable using. An exercise bike or treadmill seldom seems to attract much attention with the elderly. What does seem to work is a mild exercise program, a walking club around the facility, a van ride to a nearby mall, or a weekly dance.

For the creative people at the facility, a craft program is important. Weaving, knitting, painting, wood working, creating are all good programs for the elderly, mentally and physically. It is important that these things be encouraged and supervised. Many people do not get involved in crafts because they simply do not know how to do things. In your facility you will find people with a variety of skills and abilities. Use those who already know how to do a craft to teach those who do not. Group activities like sewing and quilting stimulate residents and enhance their psychosocial skills while involving them physically in an activity.

It is important to provide a wide variety of activities that will meet a variety of needs. For some residents, a one-on-one visit in their room is the most activity they will allow. Other residents will participate in everything. Outings are enjoyable for some, but for those who are wheel chair bound, they can be burdensome. Museums, theater and historical site visits are appropriate for some residents, but not for all. Entertainment in the facility usually draws a big crowd. Music seems to be something most residents enjoy, but it does little for the residents physically. Having food or a snack at an event seems also to bring people out of their rooms. Cookouts and parties are usually seen as special and are therefore well attended. The activity program should provide a balance between the wide options available. It is important to try to engage everyone in some activity throughout the month.

Part of what makes a successful activity program is planning. I recommend that the activity director visit each new person who comes into your facility. She should prepare an activity assessment form that gathers information about what the resident enjoyed doing before they moved into the facility as well as their current limitations. From these forms the activity director can begin to plan events that offer programs people enjoy. It is best to plan at least one month ahead. Most states require that an activity calendar be posted for each month. It is important not to deviate from the calendar. If it is unavoidable, a notice should be made or posted to inform the residents and families. Be sure the calendar lists the who, what, when and where details for each event. Place it in a location where residents and families can see it and refer to upcoming events when interacting with residents.

One important part of the activity program is volunteer recruitment. No activity staff can do everything. Develop a volunteer application that lists what the volunteer enjoys doing and how often they would like to volunteer. Some states require a criminal background test and a TB test for volunteers that come to the facility on a regular bases. Some of your best volunteers may be family members. Their volunteering often times is just as important for them as it is for the residents. Develop job descriptions for each volunteer task and review this with the volunteer to ensure that they know what is expected and are willing to do the task. Have some special name badge for volunteers and a special recognition time annually to thank them for their good work.

There are several kinds of programs I would like to recommend. The first is pet therapy animals. Pets in general are stimulating for people of all ages. The therapy dogs have had some special training and relate well to people. The residents respond well to these animals and usually look forward to the next visit. Be careful however, not everyone likes dogs! The second kind of program I would recommend is religious. The residents in your facility will have a variety of religious beliefs so not all these programs appeal to everyone. It is important to offer a variety of services. What does seem to appeal is the music. Choirs, hymn sings and concerts of religious music are very popular with older adults. The third kind of program that seems to create a lot of smiles is a relationship with a nearby elementary or preschool. Monthly visits by the children give the residents something to look forward to. The children often entertain or bring some crafts they have made. The residents can also prepare for the visits and help make cookies or gifts to give to the children.

The activity personnel who work in the nursing facilities are included in the interdisciplinary care team and are an important part of promoting a positive quality of life. They are required to chart in the resident chart regarding their ability to participate and willingness to do so. This person also is a part of the care planning team. Once important information has been gathered regarding the ability of the resident to participate in a variety of activity programs, the activity personnel are required to establish goals for this resident and to help develop a plan of care to enable the resident to participate as fully as possible. These activities are supposed to be based on the resident's needs and interest as identified in the assessment that was done upon admission. The purpose of activities for nursing facility residents is to engage residents in a social, recreational or religious function they enjoy.

The Code of Federal Regulation in section 483.15 include the following comments regarding actives:

The facility must provide for an ongoing program of activities designed to meet, in accordance with the comprehensive assessment, the interests and the physical, mental, and psychosocial well-being of each resident.

The activities program must be directed by a qualified professional who:

(i) Is a qualified therapeutic recreation specialist or an activities professional who is licensed or registered, if applicable, by the State in which practicing; and

(B) Is eligible for certification as a therapeutic recreation specialist or as an activities professional by a recognized accrediting body on or after October 1, 1990; or

(ii) Has two years of experience in a social or recreational program within the last five years, one of which was full-time in a patient activities program in a health care setting; or

(iii) Is a qualified occupational therapist or occupational therapy assistant; or

(iv) Has completed a training course approved by the State.[21]

The important thing to remember about activities is that once listed on a calendar that residents can see, they must occur at that time and on that day. Residents and families both look forward to the events happening as planned.

Chapter Eleven

Dining

Good food and good nutrition play a major part in healing and keeping people strong. Most states recommend that long-term care facilities follow a minimum standard plan in establishing their menus, such as the U.S. Department of Agriculture Food Pyramid Guide. The guide suggests that each person receive six to eleven servings of bread, cereal, rice or pasta per day, two to four servings of fruit, three to five servings of a vegetable, two to three servings of meat, poultry, fish, dry beans, eggs, or nuts, and two to three servings of milk, yogurt or cheese. Following these guidelines is a good beginning when planning a menu for elderly residents.

Selecting food menus is the first step in meeting the needs of the long-term care resident. It is therefore advisable to hire a dietician to assist in this process. It is possible to buy diets for people in this age group and setting, but a dietician is also a good person to have for special diets or consultations. Nursing homes are required to have at least a contracted person in this capacity. Most facilities establish four different menus cycles based on the seasons of the year. Once these menus are established, recipes may be purchased or produced by the dietary staff to insure the same quality and taste each time an item is prepared.

Once the menu is set, the next step is to order the food necessary to prepare the meals. It is very important to watch raw food costs as closely as possible. Often times, food is ordered by the case. Before an order is placed, be sure to count how many pieces are still on hand from the last time an item was used. For instance, if a case of 40 pieces of chicken was ordered and you only used 30 pieces, then after two more orders you should have enough of the unused pieces to meet your needs rather than order again.

It is best to establish a par level for food supplies. Many states require that you have a certain number of days of food be on hand at all times. Use this as the beginning point. Once your food supply gets below a certain level in every category, order more.

Once the food has been prepared, the next step is presentation. It is important to make the healthy food appealing. The first part of presentation is making sure the food is served at the right temperature. The adage is "serve hot food hot and cold food cold." Melted ice cream or cold mashed potatoes are not very appetizing. It is good to check the food temperature when the last resident is served to insure that the food is at an appropriate temperature. Plate presentation is also important. A little garnishment goes a long way in making the eyes think the food will be good. Taking the time to dress the plate so that foods are separated and gravy is not dripping over the side of the plate will convey a message of care and class. The wait staff should be trained in how to set, serve and clear a table as if they were serving in a restaurant. And finally, the dining environment is also important. Be sure the dining room is pleasant and bright. Soft music in the background along with flowers and table linen make for a nice atmosphere for the residents.

Dining, however, is the one area where you can please some of the people some of the time, but you cannot please all of the people all of the time. Everyone has his own food and preparation method preference. It is therefore important that the cook try to determine what kinds of food most people like and then try to prepare it. There will always be people who do not like a particular vegetable or meat, so it is always good to offer some choices.

Residents who are on a special diet for health or religious reasons should have those special diets honored. It may be that your cook may not have the ability to prepare food in a particular way. In that case, packaged meals may be an appropriate alternative. These tend to be expensive. You may want to consider this expense before admitting a resident with a special dietary need. Another suggestion is to be very frank about the added expense and charge them the difference in your normal plate costs and the costs of the special meal. If at all possible, it is best to honor dietary requests.

If residents do have special dietary needs, the dietician should be consulted and the proper diet provided. Types of special diets include a low sodium diet that are normally for people with heart problems or with high blood pressure, a low fat diet for people with high cholesterol, a high protein for people who need to build body tissue, a diabetic diet for diabetics, a liquid diet for residents post surgery and a bland diet for people with ulcers.

Using left over food is a good way to cut costs. Once an item is served to a resident, it cannot be returned to the kitchen. However, left over meats or vegetables that have not been served can be used to make homemade soups, salads or casseroles. Be sure the menu allows you to serve beef stew or chicken salad after you have offered pot roast or baked chicken. These left over foods that are to be used again must be properly labeled to identify what they are and when they were placed in the cooler for reuse.

Many long-term care facilities use staff from nursing or activities to assist in meal service. In some states the Health Departments issue food handlers cards to people who have undergone a specific training that gives instruction in safe handling of food from preparation to distribution. If this is not offered, it would be good to have your food service manager give some basic instruction regarding serving and clearing of tables. It is also a good idea to have someone in the dining room that is first aid certified or at least CPR certified in the event a resident begins to choke.

Staffing is important in dining just as it is in all departments. Having too many staff working will increase dining costs and having too few employees will reduce resident satisfaction. The head cook or chef should be the person who orders the food based on the menu and the number of meals to be served. He/she is also responsible for the supervision of the rest of the staff. One cook can prepare a meal for twenty or for eighty. The difference is in the preparation. Hiring someone as a kitchen aide to help make a salad or do some of the food prep work for the next meal will make the preparation much better. The clean up after each meal can be done by a non-skilled employee, who washes pots and pan, runs the dishwasher, wipes down all surfaces, and mops the floor.

Having the right amount of food and supplies on hand is essential to a smoothly running dietary department. Set a par level for food and supplies and when the food amount available gets to that level, order more. Having a set par level will also make it easy to determine what must be ordered to meet the menu and what should be left in reserve for an emergency. The problem occurs when the supplier runs out of an item and the cook needs to use something else. That means that the potatoes that were intended for another meal are being used early.

It is best to try to stay with the posted menu. People do not like to come to a meal and be surprised at what they find. Some facilities put out a weekly menu and ask resident to review it and decide what they would like based on the options available. Others post a monthly menu but do not ask until the day before what the residents would like to eat. The more control you have on how many meals are being served, the better the food costs will be. Asking the residents to indicate what selections they would like, in advance of a meal will help with portion control. A common problem in selecting meals ahead of time is that people sometimes change their minds! The nursing homes and most assisted living facilities are required to keep copies of their menus and to note any changes on the menus posted if any changes are necessary.

Options are important on menus. It is not necessary to have six different entrees for each meal, but at least two choices with a variety of substitutes like salads or soups are appreciated. Offering several vegetables with each meal will also address the issue of not having carrots often enough or having them too often.

The local Health Department inspects all dining establishments. They most often have a checklist of things they look for and a rating scale to help determine how well the inspection went. The checklist may look something like this:

YES	NO	
		Hand wash sink available and clean?
		Soap in hand wash dispenser?
		Paper towels available near hand wash sink?
		Trash can available near hand wash sink?
		Employee rest room available for Dietary personnel?
		Employee restroom clean and free from odors?
		Food is stored properly, off the floor?
		Food, once opened has been rewrapped and dated?
		Correct water temperatures in the dishwasher to insure that the boosters are washing and rinsing at the correct temperature?
		Correct food handling procedures used to insure there is no contamination?
		Pests or rodents in the kitchen or storage areas?
		Fans, lights, floors, hood filters and equipment are clean?
		Lights above the stove and cooking surfaces working and the glass cover is clean and firmly in place?
		Stored canned goods will be inspected for dents and missing labels?
		Storage areas will be inspected to make sure chemical products are not stored above food products?
		Dry goods that have scoops will be inspected to insure that a lid is on top of the container and that the scoop inside has the handle up?
		Trash cans/ dumpsters clean and odor free?
		Food temperatures within appropriate range as served?
		Hair nets and gloves worn as required?
		Appropriate ventilation?
		Doors and windows have screens or knock down fans to prevent flying?
		Food prep area clean?
		Wipe clothes in bleach solution when not in use?

The rating scale will help track what improvements need to be made to keep the kitchen clean and functioning within certain standards.

The food storage and preparation and serving environment must be kept clean at all times. The reason is to prevent any food borne illnesses. Foods like fish, meat, poultry and eggs should be handled with care. They should be refrigerated or frozen upon delivery. None of these products should get above 41 degrees Fahrenheit. If the foods are frozen, they need to remain below 0 degree Fahrenheit.

Likewise, the cleaning of dishes, utensils and equipment is also important. The use of chemicals in the typical three compartment sink and high temperatures in the automatic dishwashers both help to serve this purpose. The dishwashers must produce water at 140 degrees Fahrenheit in the wash cycle and 180 degrees Fahrenheit in the rinse cycle to meet regulations.

Dining is an important department. Having the right personnel in this department can save money and keep residents happy.

Sec. 483.35 Of the Code of Federal Regulations identifies theses specific regulations regarding Dietary services in nursing facilities.

The facility must provide each resident with a nourishing, palatable, well-balanced diet that meets the daily nutritional and special dietary needs of each resident.

(a) Staffing. The facility must employ a qualified dietitian either full-time, part-time, or on a consultant basis.

(1) If a qualified dietitian is not employed full-time, the facility must designate a person to serve as the director of food service who receives frequently scheduled consultation from a qualified dietitian.

(2) A qualified dietitian is one who is qualified based upon either registration by the Commission on Dietetic Registration of the American Dietetic Association, or on the basis of education, training, or experience in identification of dietary needs, planning, and implementation of dietary programs.

(b) Sufficient staff. The facility must employ sufficient support personnel competent to carry out the functions of the dietary service.

(c) Menus and nutritional adequacy. Menus must:

(1) Meet the nutritional needs of residents in accordance with the recommended dietary allowances of the Food and Nutrition Board of the National Research Council, National Academy of Sciences;

(2) Be prepared in advance; and

(3) Be followed.

(d) Food. Each resident receives and the facility provides:

(1) Food prepared by methods that conserve nutritive value, flavor, and appearance;

(2) Food that is palatable, attractive, and at the proper temperature;

(3) Food prepared in a form designed to meet individual needs; and

(4) Substitutes offered of similar nutritive value to residents who refuse food served.

(e) Therapeutic diets. The attending physician must prescribe therapeutic diets.

(f) Frequency of meals.

(1) Each resident receives and the facility provides at least three meals daily, at regular times comparable to normal mealtimes in the community.

(2) There must be no more than 14 hours between a substantial evening meal and breakfast the following day, except as provided in (4) below.

(3) The facility must offer snacks at bedtime daily.

(4) When a nourishing snack is provided at bedtime, up to 16 hours may elapse between a substantial evening meal and breakfast the following day if a resident group agrees to this meal span, and a nourishing snack is served.

(g) Assistive devices. The facility must provide special eating equipment and utensils for residents who need them.

(h) Paid feeding assistants:

(1) State-approved training course. A facility may use a paid feeding assistant, as defined in Sec. 488.301 of this chapter, if:

(i) The feeding assistant has successfully completed a State-approved training course that meets the requirements of Sec. 483.160 before feeding residents; and

(ii) The use of feeding assistants is consistent with state law.

Supervision.

(i) A feeding assistant must work under the supervision of a registered nurse (RN) or licensed practical nurse (LPN).

(ii) In an emergency, a feeding assistant must call a supervisory nurse for help on the resident call system.

(3) Resident selection criteria.

(i) A facility must ensure that a feeding assistant feeds only residents who have no complicated feeding problems.

(ii) Complicated feeding problems include, but are not limited to, difficulty swallowing, recurrent lung aspirations, and tube or parenteral/IV feedings.

(iii) The facility must base resident selection on the charge nurse's assessment and the resident's latest assessment and plan of care.

(i) Sanitary conditions. The facility must

(1) Procure food from sources approved or considered satisfactory by federal, state, or local authorities;

(2) Store, prepare, distribute, and serve food under sanitary conditions; and

(3) Dispose of garbage and refuse properly."[22]

.

Chapter Twelve

Finance

The administrator is responsible for the finances of the facility. Everything from billing residents to petty cash is ultimately the responsibility of the person in charge. The size of the facility will determine how much of the accounting services are performed on site. In some cases, a company may have multiple facilities and use accounting personnel at the home office to perform the majority of the work involved in billing and paying bills. This is called accounts receivable and accounts payable in business terms. Often times these functions are divided between a bookkeeper who records the daily cash transactions of money in and money out and the accountant who puts together financial reports based on the information supplied by the bookkeeper. The administrator may perform some or all of these functions himself if they are in a small assisted living facility, or may directly or indirectly supervise others who do this work. In either case, it is the responsibility of the administrator to understand enough about finances to be able to use the information the accounting staff provides to make informed decisions about the facility. It is his/her responsibility to assure that enough income is available to conduct business, to buy the supplies necessary, to pay wages and to make mortgage payments. By being fully informed of how much income to expect through the resident billing, the administrator will be able to make wise decisions on what expenses the facility can endure at any given time. If income from resident billing is not sufficient to meet expenses, the facility will not be able to continue on for very long. It is therefore very important to know how to set rates for the services provided and to budget for expenses anticipated. Setting rates that are too high may drive away current or potential customers. Setting them too low may mean a loss of potential income that could be used in a variety of ways to benefit the facility or the residents. Budgeting too high for services may require you to raise rent rates that cause dissatisfaction among the residents. It is very important that the administrator know as much as possible about finances to insure that the facility budgets properly, spends only what it can pay for and retains residents who pay for the services rendered.

Regardless of how the facility is set up, there are terms and principles that the administrator must understand to be successful.

Definitions:

Accounting: a service activity that provides quantitative information about economic entities; the information is financial in nature and is intended to be useful in making economic decisions.

Assets: probable future economic benefits obtained or controlled by a particular entity as a result of past transactions of events.

Balance Sheet: a financial report showing assets, liabilities and equity on a given date.

Credit: the right side of a T-account, or entries that decrease assets, or increase liabilities or equity.

Debit: the left side of a T-account, or entries that increase assets, decrease liabilities or equity.

Equity: the residual interest in the assets of an entity that remains after deducting its liabilities.

Expense: outflows, the using up of assets or the incurrence of liabilities as a result of the central operations of a business.

GAAP: an acronym for Generally Accepted Accounting Principles.

General Ledger: the ledger containing the financial statement accounts of a business.

Income Statement: a financial statement showing revenues earned.

Liabilities: probable future sacrifices of economic benefits arising from present obligations of a particular entity to transfer assets or provide services to other entities in the future as the result of past transactions or events.

Revenue: an inflow of assets received in exchange for services provided to customers as part of the major operations of the business.

Statement of Cash Flows: a financial statement that discloses the cash inflows and outflow from operations, investments and financing.

The accounting process involves many steps, but they can be narrowed into two primary steps. The first is keeping the books and the second is preparing the financial statements. In booking, someone records all revenue (income) and expenses (outflow) during a particular time frame, usually a month.

There are two different types of accounting, cash basis and accrual. Cash basis accounting is the form used to balance a personal checkbook. It's also the form of accounting used to pay individual income tax. Revenues or deposits are recognized in the checkbook when one actually receives cash or deposits cash in the bank account. Expenses are recognized when cash is paid, such as when a check is written or cash is withdrawn. Accrual basis accounting is an adjustment process used to record revenue and expense in the period in which they are earned or incurred. The primary benefit to the accrual basis of accounting is that it allows for easier comparability of statements of different periods. An example of how this can be beneficial is that for some reason, the cable TV bill is late. The cable bill is the same each month. The accountant can accrue for this bill rather than pay twice as much the following month. A second example may be employee insurance. The bills for this insurance may come twice a year. Rather than pay a large sum twice a year, the accountant can accrue a percentage each month to be able to have enough when the bill comes. Generally accepted accounting principles are based on the concept of accrual basis accounting.

There are two functions in accounting, recording and preparing financial statements. These financial statements include a variety of accounts. They are organized into these five groups: assets, liabilities, capital, revenues, and expenses. Each of these accounts has a number.

Most often, the Assets accounts would include things like Petty Cash, Checking-Operations, Checking-payroll, Savings, accounts receivable from Residents rent, building, furniture, vehicles, land, depreciation etc. Beside each name would be the corresponding number for that account.

The Liabilities account would include account payable items like trade. There would also be accrued payroll, payroll clearing, federal, state and local taxes withheld from payroll, employee savings, retirement savings, garnishments withheld etc.

Capital accounts include moneys invested in the facility. This would be equipment, furnishings and major appliances. Many companies have a minimum dollar value that helps define what a capital expenditure is compared to a normal purchase from the operations budget.

The *Revenue account* lists revenue from resident billing, money from employee meals, nursing supplies sold to the resident and any income from services provided to the residents.

The *Expense account* is usually the largest because it includes wages, payroll taxes, employee's benefits and expenses around recruiting and training employees for each department in the building. These departments are generally broken down into administration, building, dietary, housekeeping, and nursing. Beyond these common line items that are found in each department, there are also items like supplies, newspaper and magazine subscriptions, insurance, audit and legal fees, postage, marketing, real estate taxes and telephone in Administration, auto expense, disposal, maintenance repair, snow removal and utilities under building, food, consultants rental under dietary, cleaning and laundry supplies under housekeeping, and activities, outside labor, professional fees and consultants under nursing.

The following is an example of the chart of accounts along with the numbers that are associated with them.

Operating Expense

Nursing Services
613110: Wages & Management
613120: Wages & LPN's
613140: Wages & CNA's
613150: Wages & Holiday/vacation pay
613160: Contract Labor

Payroll Taxes and Employees Benefits
613210: Payroll Taxes–FICA
613220: Payroll Taxes–FUI
613230: Payroll Taxes–SUI
613240: Group Health Insurance
Supplies
613310: Medical supplies–billable
613320: Medical supplies–non-billable
613330: Minor equipment
613340: Supplies

Any transaction, either money in or money out, will affect some account. The journals are the place where these transactions are recorded. In the smaller facilities, money may be deposited in the bank and the record of that deposit sent to a corporate office where the bookkeeper enters information in the journal. Bills may also be paid out of a corporate office, where once again, the transaction is noted. Most facilities allow the administrator to control a petty cash account to pay for small items rather than send purchase orders to the home office. These small payments are recorded and sent to the bookkeeper to be recorded in the appropriate journal. If the building is large enough, this book work is done on site. The use of credit cards enables the facility to buy materials on line but can also be abused easily.

Generally, there are six journals. They are:

Billings Journal: this one lists all bills sent for services rendered. This includes primarily bills sent to residents for their monthly rent and services.

Cash Receipts Journal: this records all payments received for any services provided and any sales made. This would include monthly rental fees, payments for supplies used like diapers and any other charges billed to the residents for services or supplies.

Accounts Payable Journal: this is a record of all the purchases made that will be paid in the near future. Supplies is an area that can easily get out of hand. This journal tells you all the payments that were made and to whom for the month. The only thing not included here is payroll.

Cash Disbursements Journal: this is a record of all the payments that were made for services or supplies to care for the residents. A review of this journal will help you keep within budget each month.

Payroll Journal: this one summarizes all payroll checks distributed during the month. A print out should be provided to the administrator for each pay period and one for the month. This journal can be helpful in making sure overtime is kept within budget.

General Journal: this is a record of non-repetitive entries. In this journal, transactions are recorded that do not fit into any of the other five journals. Adjustments in the books are made by virtue of this journal to help make sure they conform to the accrual system of accounting.

Double entry accounting is the normal formula of accounting. In this case, each transaction has two entries, one on the left side of the journal as a debit and one on the right side of the journal as a credit. At the end of the month, the left and right side should be even. An example might be when a bill is sent to a resident, the amount on the bill is listed in the appropriate journal as a debit. When the bill is paid, that same amount is listed as a credit.

All the entries should have a source document associated with it. This could be a bill from a vendor, a check request form completed for petty cash, a purchase approval form complete with a bill to be paid. Many companies like to pay from invoices rather than wait for bills. In this case the invoices are submitted when the product is received. Be sure to compare the invoice with the bill when it comes. All these source documents should come through the administrator before they go to the accounting personnel.

The General Ledger is the place where once a month all the journals have posted their information. It is the one report the administrator can review that includes all debits and credits for the month. This is of tremendous value when preparing a monthly management report if one is required. If not, it is a good source of information that enables the administrator to know in detail what has transpired financially over the past month. The General Ledger also normally provides a comparison of debits and credits to what has been budgeted. In addition, it also provides year to date information that can help the administrator make sure that he/she is on track or to make plans to get on track to meet the budget for the year.

There are three statements that are produced once the General Ledger is completed. The first is the *Income Statement*. This tells the administrator whether the revenues were enough to cover the expenses. The typical accounting understanding of income is not simply the money that comes into the facility, but revenues minus expenses. Net income means the facility brought in more than it spent and net loss means just the opposite. The goal is to have a net income.

The second statement produced from the General Ledger is the *Balance Sheet*. This statement is a summary of the assets, liabilities and capital accounts. The standard formula for this is that assets are equal to liabilities plus capital. Assets are the things the facility owns that can be sold or turned into cash somehow within twelve months. Liabilities are those bills that must be paid within the next twelve months. This includes utilities, food, nursing supplies, anything that must be paid within a year. Capital includes money invested in the facility by the owner along with any net income that has been put back into the facility.

The *Statement of Change* indicates the transactions that occurred over the past month. It would show how the amount of working capital has changed over the month and why.

It is important that the administrator understand these various statements that are produced by the accountant. They provide a concise picture of the financial health of the facility.

Besides the accounting statements there are a few reports that are helpful to the administrator in keeping on top of facility costs. The first is the *daily census*. This tells the administrator every day how many people are in the facility. By reviewing this information, the administrator should be able to compare that number to a budgeted number to give him/her a ballpark idea of how much revenue they can expect. The second is an *overtime work report*. If the administrator gets this each week, he/she can make necessary changes in the schedule as quickly as possible. Keeping over time down will be one of the biggest ways to stay within the budget. The third report that is quick and very helpful is an *ageing report*. This report tells the administrator who has not paid their bill. By acting on this report quickly with a phone call, letters, registered mail or whatever the policies allow, the facility can get the money owed faster. Every day of lost revenue has a negative impact on the facility.

Preparing a budget is a difficult but essential job. It should begin with a clear understanding of what the business would like to accomplish in the year ahead. This requires a strategic plan that is usually written for three to five years ahead. It has listed three to four goals and objectives that are most essential. The budget should clearly show that the administrator has chosen to put money into the projects that are of most significance according to the strategic plan. The management plan and the marketing plan should serve as the cornerstones for developing the operating budget. There should also be a capital budget prepared that indicates what projects will be undertaken in the year ahead. Does the building need a new roof? Are room renovations required? Is there a need for new lobby furniture? The capital budget is a way of setting money aside for major expenditures that require attention. Once the strategic plan and the capital budget have been reviewed, then it is time to begin operating budget preparations. When doing so, the administrator can do it or ask for input from the Department Directors. If the facility is organized using the team concept, it makes good sense to have the team leaders or department director, participate in the budget preparation. One of the advantages of a budget prepared with input from the team leaders is that they become aware of all the components of the budget, the anticipated income as well as the anticipated expenses. They become more informed and can serve as an ally when issues of salary, and benefits come up within their department. Being aware of the cost of workers compensation insurance, employee benefits, office supplies, heating and water can give the team leaders a better appreciation for how the building runs and how much it cost to do so. Another advantage of department director participation is that it allows for communication between the leaders and participation in decision-making around very important issues. If each department director is asked to submit a budget for their department, then when all budgets are submitted, the team could decide what the priorities are for the facility.

There are several steps that one must go through when establishing a budget.

1. Be aware of what the competition is doing. Check to see what the assisted living facility or nursing home down the street is paying their staff. Call some competitors and ask for information about rates and services. Be aware of any regulatory changes that may affect the facility. An example of this is the nursing facilities in Virginia were given a break in the reimbursement rate from Medicaid that they could pass along as an increase in CNA wages. The assisted living facilities did not get this kind of break. As a result the nursing faculties could and did offer a dollar more per hour to new employees. To compete, the assisted living facilities had to do the same thing. That one dollar cost the average facility of eight CNA's around the clock $70,080.00. Most facilities cannot afford to lose $70,000 a year. Be aware of new competition. Even if your facility is the best in the community, you will lose some current residents and potential residents when a new one opens.

2. Establish objectives so that money can be set aside to meet them. An example of this is when a new facility is opened. Obviously, the most important objective for that first year is to fill up the building. The budget should then allow for extra money for marketing during that year. Once it is full, the major objective can change to providing excellent care. The money set aside for marketing can be cut back some to allow for additional training for nurses, additional activities staff, or whatever is needed to provide excellent service. Maybe the building is full and has a waiting list. It may be time to add on a wing. The budget would reflect the need for more staff along with the additional amount for loan repayment for the construction. Additional supplies may also be required. By including information in the budgeting process about the facility objectives, appropriate funds will be set aside to meet these objectives.

3. Determine how much revenue to expect. It helps to be aware of the daily census, anticipating growth or decline based on the information from step one and adding up the amount of rent to be charged in the months ahead. Revenue may also be received from other sources, such as nursing supplies sold to residents, employee meals, snack machine proceeds, and furniture rental or whatever way you normally make money. List all of these sources. Estimate the amount of revenue to be earned from these sources and total them by month and finally by year.

4. Determine expenses. These include wages, benefits, cost of recruitment, taxes, workers compensation, retirement programs, mortgage payments, supplies, rental for equipment, membership dues, insurance, legal and professional fees, postage, marketing expenses, real estate taxes, phone, auto expenses, trash removal, grounds, Cable TV, snow removal, utilities, food, activities, and contract labor. When determining these expenses, be sure to add a percentage for the cost of inflation. Add these figures together and total them by month and by year. Then, compare the total expenses and your total revenue. The revenue should be greater than the expenses. If it is not you can either plan to increase the rent charged the residents or cut back on the expenses. It may be that a little of both are required.

Once the budget is set, stay within it. Do not spend more than budgeted. It is always better to have more revenue than expense!

Payroll
When hiring new employees, certain information is needed in order to process their payroll. On a form of some type should be their:
Full name
Address
Phone number
Social Security number
Rate of pay

In addition, you will need:
Federal W-4 form
The State Equivalent of the W-4 form
I-9 form
Insurance Enrollment form
Retirement form
Miscellaneous voluntary deduction forms

These are one time or perhaps annual forms. Beside these, weekly, or bi-weekly time cards of some type are also required. The electronic time systems do a very good job of counting hours and enable you to edit time if necessary. They may also produce a weekly or daily overtime report that will enable the administrator to curtail over time hours worked. Punch clocks require that someone, usually the administrator, count the time and send it in to the bookkeeper to process. It is very important that this time be accurate.

The bookkeeper will write the check after determining how much to deduct for taxes and other withholdings. It is their job to pay these taxes, social security, insurance companies and pension programs in a timely manner.

It is important to keep a copy of the punch times to be able to answers questions that come up on payday.

Employees normally get paid every two weeks. The advantage of this system for the employer is that revenue can be invested and produce higher returns if taken out every two weeks as opposed to every week. It is also important to note that the whole payroll process of adding hours, if done by hand, or reviewing clock reports, if done electronically, occurs every two weeks rather than every week, thus saving time. When setting up pay days, it is important to allow some turn around time from the end of the pay period until the day the employees are paid. As an example, if the pay period is Monday through Sunday, the payday may be the following Thursday or Friday.

Most employees will be hourly employees. That is to say, they are paid an hourly rate. For overtime purposes, an hourly employee must be paid the overtime rate after eight hours in a given day and after forty hours in a given week. Some of the employees will be salaried employees. Normally those people who are salary employees are those in management. In this case, they get paid the same amount each pay, regardless of how many hours they work.

Payroll is one of the largest expenses in the facility. Controlling the payroll is very important. It is essential that you do not have more people working at one time than is necessary. It is also important to have enough people working so that the resident's needs are being met. By hiring full time, part time and PRN employees, the department directors will be flexible enough to fill the gaps that may arise in the daily work schedule. Always make it a practice to replace someone who is ill with a part time or PRN employee in an effort to cut down on overtime. Using employees from an agency seldom is beneficial. They do not know the residents, the facility policies or the emergency procedures. It creates ill will with the staff if the agency nurses are paid more that they are getting and the agency nurse requires extra supervision.

It is important to understand and to control the payroll. Unlike the mortgage, the payroll is one of the costs that can be controlled. This control begins with establishing a par level for the number of employees needed to care for the residents. Determine how much nursing staff is necessary for each resident. A good average is about ten to one. Schedule the nursing staff around this or another resident to staff ratio. The same should be done for each department. Determine how many housekeepers will be needed by deciding how often they will required to clean each room, the common areas and offices. Most assisted living facilities have the rooms cleaned once per week with daily touch up and trash removal. Nursing homes have their room's cleaned everyday. Twenty to thirty minutes per room is a pretty standard time allotted for this service. Determine how many cooks it will take to prepare a meal. What will they do in between meals? In large communities there may be dietary aides who wash the dishes and cooks who cook the meals. Smaller ones may ask the cook to also clean up after each meal. During down time the cook could order food, scrub the floor, prep for the next meal or do some housekeeping.

It is always wise to cross train the staff. During slow times, have the nurse aides do some laundry or assist with meal service or activities. The more productive the staff can be, the more money will be saved and the better the service will be for the residents.

In addition to all the things mentioned above, nursing homes usually have some form of residents' account available for the residents. In this regard, the facility acts as a bank. The Code of Federal Regulation in section 483.10 refers to these accounts when they talk about one of the established resident rights. It is that the resident has the right to manage his or her financial affairs, and the facility may not require residents to deposit their personal funds with the facility. The management of the funds of those who have decided to let the facility serve as their bank is very important. Upon written authorization of a resident, the facility must hold, safeguard, manage, and account for the personal funds of the resident deposited with the facility. The facility must deposit any residents' personal funds in excess of $50 in an interest bearing account (or accounts) that is separate from any of the facility's operating accounts, and that credits all interest earned on resident's funds to that account. (In pooled accounts, there must be a separate accounting for each resident's share.) The facility must maintain a resident's personal funds that do not exceed $50 in a non-interest bearing account, interest-bearing account, or petty cash fund.

Once the funds are deposited, the facility is responsible for establishing and maintaining a system that assures a full and complete and separate accounting, according to generally accepted accounting principles, of each resident's personal funds entrusted to the facility on the resident's behalf. Whatever system is adopted, it should preclude any commingling of resident funds with facility funds or with the funds of any person other than another resident. There should be an individual financial record be available through quarterly statements and on request to the resident or his or her legal representative. The facility must notify each resident that receives Medicaid benefits when the amount in the resident's account reaches $200 less than the SSI resource limit for one person and that, if the amount in the account, in addition to the value of the resident's other nonexempt resources, reaches the SSI resource limit or when the resident may lose eligibility for Medicaid or SSI. Upon the death of a resident, the facility must convey within 30 days the resident's funds, and a final accounting of those funds, to the individual or probate jurisdiction administering the resident's estate. In an effort to protect itself and secure the resident funds, the facility should purchase a surety bond. These services are something the nursing facility provides free of charge. However, the facility may charge the resident for requested services that are more expensive than or in excess of covered services in accordance with Sec. 489.32 of the Nursing Facility regulations.[23]

Having a firm grasp of finances will be a great asset to the administrator. If that is not a strength, be sure to hire a good book keeper who can provide some on-the-job-training. The more you understand about making and spending money, the better able you will be in directing the business of the long-term care facility.

Chapter Thirteen

Housekeeping

Housekeeping is an integral service in a long-term care facility. When someone is looking for a facility, they look to see if it is clean and they smell to see if there are any unpleasant odors. Keeping the facility looking and smelling clean is not an easy job. It requires employees who enjoy and take pride in their work, a good plan for what will be done daily and the proper supplies and equipment to do a good job. Keeping the bathrooms, common areas, and resident rooms clean is a good foundation for an infection control program.

Work Schedule

Arrange the work schedule so that the resident rooms are cleaned at least weekly in assisted living facilities and daily in nursing homes. It is best if the cleaning can be done on the same day each week. This allows the residents a routine and notice that the housekeeper will be coming on a particular day.

Allow approximately 30 minutes to clean a bathroom and a one-bedroom suite. This includes dusting and vacuuming the bedroom area and cleaning the bathroom. One of the problems encountered in assisted living facilities is that often residents want to bring in all their possessions and try to cram them into one room. The rooms get cluttered and it makes it difficult to clean.

In most resident rooms there will be: a bed, a table near the bed, a lamp on the table, a comfortable chair, drawer space, a mirror, window coverings, and adequate wardrobe space. In some assisted living facilities and residential communities, residents are permitted to bring in some of their own furniture. In that case be sure the furniture is free of pests and that it is made from flame retardant materials. The facility should provide or at least launder sheets, pillowcases, blankets, bedspreads, towels, washcloths, and waterproof mattresses covers when needed. These can be cleaned once per week unless an accident occurs that requires more frequent cleaning. In nursing homes, cleaning should be done every day in order to keep the room odor and infection free.

Besides cleaning the rooms, it is also important to clean hallways and common areas. Hallways should be mopped one half at a time to allow people to use the other side. Use of wet floor signs are required to prevent falls on floors while they dry. Floors should be clean, but avoid using high gloss wax on tile floors to reduce glare. A weekly cleaning for common areas is appropriate but the need for touch up cleaning is constant.

Try to develop a schedule for things like carpet cleaning, window washing and stripping off old wax and applying new to tile floors.

In the long-term care industry, there is always turn over of rooms when residents are compelled to move to a higher level of care or die. Time should be built into the work schedule for occasional room turn over. It is important to respect the fact that families may be in mourning if their loved one has died or in a crises if their loved one has moved to a nursing facility, however, every day a room is vacant, the facility is losing money from room rental. The contract the residents sign should state clearly how many days after a room is vacated the families have to remove personnel belongings. It is important to stick to this so rooms can be cleaned, carpets scrubbed, walls painted and repairs made to enable the room to be rented once again.

The following is an example of a room readiness form that can be used to insure that the room is in good shape for marketing to show and sell.

Room Number:	Inspected by:	Date:		
Area/Item			Needs work	OK
Carpet				
Bathroom floor				
Tub/ shower				
Sink				
Toilet				
Walls				
Windows				
Electrical outlets				
Heat/ AC				
Cable				
Lights				
Call bell				
Door lock				

By asking housekeeping to complete this form, the administrator will then be able to decide what steps to take to have the room ready for marketing. It may be that the room needs new carpeting, window replacement or new paint. The administrator will know how much money is available in the capital improvement budget to have major repairs made or who to contact for new carpet or paint.

Supplies

All cleaning supplies should be stored in a locked area. Many kinds of cleaning supplies can be harmful if misused. Be sure the housekeeper reads the product labels and the Material Safety Data Sheets (MSDS) the company supplies. Keep a book that includes all of the Material Safety Data Sheets accessible. These sheets have emergency phone numbers on them. Any chemical used in the facility should have a corresponding MSDS sheet in that book. If an employee sprays something in their eye, the MSDS sheet will tell you what to do or where to call for an answer. Use chemicals as directed and do not mix chemicals. Make sure the housekeeping cart can be locked so that demented residents do not swallow a pretty pink liquid that may look enticing but be harmful.

The typical supplies needed are a window/glass cleaner, furniture polish, a toilet bowl cleaner, a hard surface cleaner for bathtubs and sinks and one designed for tile floors. Most long-term care facilities provide an adequate supply of toilet tissue, and soap for each bathroom. Make sure these cleaners are also antibacterial. Mop water used in one bathroom should not be used on the next. Change out the mop water and rinse out the mop after each room. Most large chemical companies have dispensing stations that hold all the chemicals you need and dispense the appropriate amount, mixed with the appropriate water ratio. This saves money and prevents accidents with chemical spills.

Equipment

A list of common equipment would include a cart that has a place on one side for a mop bucket with a wringer, a center section for chemicals, toilet paper and paper towels and a third section for trash collection. A vacuum cleaner is necessary along with extra bags. A broom and dustpan may be necessary. A dust mop to get up the dirt from tile floors along with a mop for wet floors are also necessary. Be sure to purchase wet floor signs to be used to warn people when a floor is being mopped. A shop-vac or carpet extractor that can suck up spills quickly can be very important to have in either maintenance or housekeeping.

Equipment like buffers, strippers and carpet scrubbers are nice to have, but can be rented as needed. The larger facilities will buy this equipment because they use it more often.

One way to insure that rooms are being cleaned appropriately is to develop a simple checklist that the department director or the administrator can use at the end of the day. Take the employee to one or two of the rooms they were to clean that day and check off what was to be done. Here is an example.

Employee Name
Date:
Work to be accomplished:
    Completed–
    Not completed–

Empty trash		
Replenish toilet paper/ hand towels		
Vacuum floor		
Mop bathroom floor		
Clean tub/shower		
Clean sink		
Clean toilet		
Dust furniture		

This list can be more extensive to cover the lobby and office areas. The point is that a quick sampling of the work done can lead to a positive comment on the part of the administrator about an otherwise thankless job or it can reveal that something was missed that needs attention before the end of the day.

Working in this department can be rewarding for those employees who like to see immediate progress. A floor is mopped. A spill is cleaned up. Furniture is dusted. But it can also be frustrating when just after cleaning a room, an accident occurs or someone wheels a wheelchair over the freshly mopped floor. A supportive department director that encourages patience and good work is needed in this area.

One very important responsibility of the housekeeper is to prevent the spread of infections. They should mop halls and floors with a determent germicide every day and clean resident bathrooms fixtures, hand-washing facilities in common areas and water fountains with a similar solution. Checking on soap and hand towels daily to ensure that there is an adequate supply will also be helpful in stopping the spread of infections. Dust rags and mop heads that touch surfaces should be changed frequently. Trash containers should be emptied when three quarters full and a new disposable liner inserted. Cleaning common bathrooms frequently is very important in this regard. If a resident becomes ill, cleaning their apartment with a disinfectant is essential. It is also important that mops, rags, and buckets used to clean a room where someone has been ill be cleaned with a nine to one bleach solution to ensure that viruses are killed before using the same equipment in another location.

The outside trash container is the place that is most often overlooked as a means of infection control. It is important to keep this area clean. It does not take long for rodents to find discarded food in a trash receptacle if the ground around it is littered with food and trash. This food that is not in a trash container also attracts flies that can easily make their way into the facility. The housekeeper and the dietary department should both work to keep these outside trash containers and the area around then clean. It is important to be sure the lids are on these containers at all times and that once the trash is removed, the inside of the container cleaned on a regular basis.

Some housekeepers also do laundry. It is important that resident clothes be kept clean and in good repair. Many facilities use small commercial equipment to wash resident's clothes, bed linen, and towels. This equipment normally will raise the hot water temperature to kill bacteria. Each state has it's own regulations on water temperature. Contact the Health Department for this information. Washing clothes in water too cold may not be effective and too hot may waste energy. A bleach solution may also be used in the wash to insure that clean linen is indeed clean and ready to reuse. The advantage of the commercial grade equipment is that it lasts longer. In addition, this equipment can also be connected to soap and fabric softener chemicals that in the long run are cheaper to operate than one where the correct amount of chemical is poured out and added at the appropriate time.

Contaminated linens require special handling. They should be placed in a special bag that is color-coded. This usually is red. This linen should be cleaned by itself and sterilized according the OSHA regulations to protect employees from infection.

In addition to resident clothes, table coverings and napkins should also be clean at all times. These items should be laundered separately from resident clothes. They require the use of a sanitizing agent.

The Code of Federal Regulations in section 483.70 indicates that nursing homes should provide a safe, clean, comfortable, and homelike environment, allowing the resident to use his or her personal belongings to the extent possible; housekeeping and maintenance services necessary to maintain a sanitary, orderly, and comfortable interior; clean bed and bath linens that are in good condition; private closet space in each resident room; adequate and comfortable lighting levels in all areas; comfortable and safe temperature levels and comfortable sound levels. The facility must provide each resident with:

1. A separate bed of proper size and height for the convenience of the resident;

2. A clean, comfortable mattress;

3. Bedding appropriate to the weather and climate, and;

4. Functional furniture appropriate to the resident's needs, and individual closet space in the resident's bedroom with clothes racks and shelves accessible to the resident.[24]

Chapter Fourteen

Human Resources

Human Resources is always a function of administration. Some facilities have a person working in this capacity, while others may require the administrator or secretary or some combination to perform this function. Human resources includes record keeping, recruiting, advertising, interviewing, checking records, hiring, labor relations, counseling and firing. It is important that federal and state labor laws are understood and that policies and handbooks that are written are done with these regulations in mind.

Often times, long-term care administrators are anxious to fill a position being vacated by an employee. Sometimes a poor employee is hired just to fill a hole in a schedule in the hopes they will perform well enough. But Jim Collins in his book, *Good to Great*, indicated that the CEO's that lead their companies to greatness often did just the opposite. They hired the right person and then found them a job. Collins says, "We expected that the good to great leaders would begin by setting a new vision and strategy. We found that they *first* got the right people on the bus, the wrong people off the bus, and the right people in the right seats—and then they figured out where to drive it. The old adage "People are your most important asset" turns out to be wrong. People are not your most important asset. The *right* people are."[25] This is a little harder to do in a small assisted living facility, but the concept is important to remember in hiring new employees. Hire the best person for the job, and if necessary, create a job for a good employee. In the end, that employee will help the community.

Before someone can be hired, they need to know what they are expected to do. It is important that job descriptions be accurate for the jobs that need to be done. The description should give enough information about the particular job that it is clear to all exactly what the position entails. In the description there should also be a prioritized list of job duties. It can also list the skills, education or experience required for the position.

It is important that each position within the community have a job description. If all of the care givers are certified nurse aides, then one job description will be used for all care givers. If all of the dietary aides do the same job, then one job description is sufficient, but if one does something different, then that position should have a different job description. There may end up being twelve to fifteen different job descriptions in your facility. Be sure to use it when hiring and during any disciplinary action.

A job description should include the following information:

A job title that defines the position.

A job summary that briefly defines responsibilities and working relationships.

Any educational requirements or certifications required.

A list of significant duties and responsibilities.

A place for the new employee to sign and date.

Recruitment:

There are many things that influence the ability to recruit employees for the community. The first is the *location*. If the facility is in an urban area, there are many people who live near by. If not, is the facility reachable by public transportation? Many facilities try to locate not far from a hospital, but the problem encountered there is the competition the hospital provides for employees. Some times, facilities have been open for a long time and the neighborhood that was appropriate ten years earlier is no longer a safe neighborhood for employees or residents. If the potential employee is afraid to drive into the neighborhood to apply for a job, they will certainly not become an employee.

Another factor in recruiting is the availability for *career advancement*. If an employee does not see opportunities to move from housekeeper to nurse aide to LPN, then they may take a job in an organization that does offer some mobility. Many organizations use a "hire from within" policy. That enables the organization to groom good employees for the next position up the career ladder. It also helps with employee retention.

A third factor is how job needs are *advertised*. Many people looking for jobs still read the want ads in the local paper. However, more and more people are using the web as a means of finding position openings. The Unemployment Commissions can also be a referral source. Posting job openings with schools of nursing or at local colleges will attract employees who want to stay in the area. Advertising the community for potential residents can also be an unintended means of letting potential employees know who you are and what you do.

The fourth factor in recruiting is *referrals* from family and friends. Current employees can be a wonderful source of referrals. They often times talk to family members and friends about where they work and what happens there. These employees tell others what it is like to work in the community and can be a positive influence on their friends and family members. (A word of caution is necessary here. It is NEVER a good policy to have family members supervise one another.) It is money well spent to institute an employee referral policy that rewards current employees financially for each new employee they encourage to work within the organization.

Hiring:

Hiring begins with *application review*. If the community does not have an application, the licensing board in most states can provide one. The items that are normally included in an application are:

The name and address of the facility.

A title such as Application for Employment.

A space for personal information like name, address, phone number.

The position for which the person is applying.

Part time or full time hours requested.

Questions about eligibility to work in this country.

Any limitations they may have that would prevent them from working at the job.

The following is an example of an application.

NAME:
SOCIAL SECURITY:
STREET:

CITY/TOWN:
STATE:
ZIP:
TELEPHONE NUMBER:
DATE OF BIRTH:

EMERGENCY CONTACT:
NAME:

TELEPHONE NUMBER:
ADDRESS:

PLACE OF LAST EMPLOYMENT:
EMPLOYER:
ADDRESS:
DATES EMPLOYED:
POSITION HELD:

PREVIOUS WORK EXPERIENCE:
PREVIOUS EDUCATION AND TRAINING:
ADDITIONAL REQUIREMENTS:
TWO WRITTEN REFERENCES.
AN ORIGINAL CRIMINAL RECORD CHECK

FOR ALL EMPLOYEES, REQUIRED HEALTH REPORTS.
FOR ALL EMPLOYEES, DOCUMENTATION OF FORMAL TRAINING AND EDUCATION RECEIVED FOLLOWING EMPLOYMENT.

It is ideal to review a stack of applications without seeing the applicant. Things like age, sex, and race should not be a factor when it comes to hiring. The most qualified person should be given the job. Having said that, it is true that we are influenced by many factors as we decide whom to hire. Handwriting, spelling, past places of employment, education, references and length of stay in previous jobs all influence the reviewer to go the next step of calling the applicant in for an interview. The task of the administrator or the human resources coordinator is to weed out employees they think do not fit and to prioritize the rest of the applications for interviews.

The interview is the most important step in the hiring process. This is another opportunity to prioritize the applicants for a possible employment offer. One of purposes for the interview is to clarify information on the application. It is important that time is taken to ask questions of clarification to insure that all the information on the application is correct.

There are numerous federal laws that have been enacted over the years that have an affect on this part of the hiring process. The Civil Rights Act prohibits employers from discriminating against potential employees based on race, color, religion, sex, or national origin. The Age Discrimination Act of 1978 says that applicants over 40 and under 70 are also protected from discrimination. These two acts dictate what can and cannot be asked during the interview process. Below is a list of those questions an employer cannot ask.

Do you have a disability?

Any questions about how the applicant learned how to read, speak, or write a foreign language.

Are you married? Where dose your spouse work? What are the ages of your children?

Any questions about complexion or color of skin.

Names, address, ages etc. of the applicant's children or relatives.

Any questions about the religious affiliation of the applicant.

Questions about any military service.

Question about the age of the applicant.

Questions about national origin.

Questions about citizenship.

Questions about social organizations to which they may belong.

Have you ever been arrested?

The following are questions an employer can ask:

What are your present or past job duties?

What progress did you make while working at your last position?

Why did you leave your last job?

Why are you looking for another job?

What experience do you have working with the elderly?

Have you ever been convicted of a crime?

Are you subject to any pending criminal charges?

Are you legally eligible to work in the United States?

Do you have any physical limitations that prevent you from performing the essential duties of the position for which you are applying?

Be sure to keep a checklist in front of you while you interview so that you do not ask the wrong questions. If the applicant does not get the job you could end up in a law suite.

Once you have satisfied all of your questions from the application, the next step is to get to know more about the potential employee. There are many types of interviewing methods. Basically, they come down to directive and non-directive. The directive method is one that insures that all of the applicants answer the same question. So, a list is prepared ahead of time and questions are asked in an effort to gather as much information as possible. Open-ended questions provide the applicant an opportunity to sell himself to the interviewer. Questions like, "What do you enjoy most about nursing?" allow the applicant to tell you more than they could in the application. The non-directive method is a little more freewheeling and casual. This allows the applicant to be comfortable and express things they may not in the more formal directed approach.

Weather the directive or non-directive method is used, some of the questions that are asked should allow the applicant to answer how they would handle a hypothetical situation. This is called behavioral interviewing. "Tell me about a time when..." usually enables the interviewer to learn a great deal about the applicant. It gives them freedom to explain a situation, how they handled it, and what they would do differently now.

To get valid information from the person being interviewed and keep the interview on track, try to follow these suggestions:

Keep questions brief, specific, and in the past tense.

Ask questions that force the person being interviewed to give the details of what he/she actually did or said in a given situation.

Ask follow up questions to bring out the details or to keep the person being interviewed on track.

Don't suggest examples or ideas of your own.

Don't accept generalizations or one-word answers. Ask the candidate to tell you more about what happened.

Get the whole story. Ask about the situation, what was happening, what was said and done and the result of comments or actions.

If the person being interviewed can't think of an event like the one you are looking for, ask several questions to help bring out an answer.

Ask what the person was thinking, why they decided to act one way or another.

Stay neutral. Don't give the candidate feedback on your opinions about their answers. This could steer the candidate and contaminate the data you are collecting.

Once the interview is over, reference checks need to be made on past employment history and especially reason for discharge. If this goes well, some communities require drug-screening test and most states require TB screening before the employee is hired. Some communities give written competency tests for some positions to determine if the applicant is knowledgeable in their area of expertise. A secretary may be required to type sixty words per minute or to be proficient in certain computer programs before they are hired. Nurses could be issued written exams to determine their knowledge base. So long as all applicants for a particular job are asked to take the same test, this is an appropriate method of eliminating unqualified candidates. Retain the results of all of these tests for the personnel files. Some states require you to separate any medical information for the rest of the file. In this case the result of TB tests or drug screening should be kept in a separate place from the application and reference check results.

Many states also require a criminal record check prior to hiring an employee. Since these records are obtained through a law enforcement agency, such as the state police, a sworn disclosure statement is required to enable the facility to hire someone before the police investigation is complete. This statement says something like "the laws of this state prohibit long-term care facilities from hiring individuals convicted of the following: murder, manslaughter, malicious wounding etc." The potential employee signs the form indicating that he/she has not been convicted of any of the listed crimes. There needs to be a statement that says any falsification of the information provided will result in the loss of employment.

Some positions require a check of license. For instance, nurses, certified nurse aides, administrators and social workers commonly have a license. The states usually provide a way to check to see if the license is valid.

All potential employees should have references that can be called to verify that the person is the best candidate for the position for which they have applied. If at all possible, call the current or previous employer for this information. A friend or family member will seldom give a bad reference.

When all of the interviews and tests are complete and an applicant has been selected for a particular position, he/she should be informed in writing or in person. Be sure to share the job description, the salary they will be paid, the starting date and a list of benefits they will be eligible to receive.

If the candidate accepts the offer of employment, there should be an orientation program designed to help them learn about the policies and procedures of your particular community. It seems to work well to have employees buddy up for a few days in an effort to have a good employee explain how things are done and why. Studies have shown that the longer the orientation process before someone is given full responsibility, the longer the person stays employed. It costs a great deal to advertise, screen and orient a new employee. The less often you are required to do this, the better it is for the community and the residents.

The candidates, who have had an interview but have not been chosen for the position, should be notified. Their applications should be retained for another position if they are interested. Many times a new employees simply does not work out. Notifying the candidate who was the second choice about the opening may enable you to skip the advertising process again.

Staffing

The Health Care Finance Administration (HCFA) requires that the number of nursing hours per resident per day stipulated to meet the resident's needs be provided in nursing homes. Some states set a specific minimum while others do not. The administrator needs to inquire from the state to determine the minimum nursing staffing level. Staffing at less than this number will result in a deficiency during the annual inspection, even if patient care is good.

One of the jobs of the administrator is to forecast. It is true in hiring staff for the facility. Determine how many staff members are needed to provide good care and meet the state minimums.

When planning staffing needs, plan around full time equivalents (FTE's). It takes 1.4 FTE's to have an LPN on the unit working the 7-3 shift seven days per week. Multiplied by three shifts, it takes 4.2 FTE's. This means that for that position, three full time nurses working forty hours per week and three part time nurses are required. In planning staffing, allow for additional part time staff to be able to come in when some calls out sick or takes a vacation or is called for jury duty. Having a large part time poll helps keep overtime down because it allows the scheduler to call upon an employee to fill a hole in the schedule without paying overtime.

Although HCFA does not specify the number of personnel needed to staff a facility, it sets standards for all personnel involved in resident care as well as some other personnel.

These are required positions: the administrator must be licensed by the state that determines the qualifications for licensing. The medical director is a physician who gives guidance to the nursing staff. They are normally part time and can be a physician who has patients in the facility. Some states require these physicians to have special qualifications or licenses to serve in this capacity. The nursing staff in skilled nursing facilities and nursing facilities are required to be sufficient to provide nursing and related service for attaining and maintaining the highest practicable physical, mental and psychosocial well being of the residents. Sufficient means that the nursing staff on duty will always be able to provide the care outlined in the resident care plans. The director of nursing is a registered nurse in nursing homes. On her days off, another registered nurse must be on duty. The charge nurse is either an RN or LPN. They are responsible for a unit and report to the director of nursing. There must be a charge nurse on duty each shift. Other nurses may serve in a variety of functions, such as the MDS coordinator, the wound care nurse, the infection control nurse, the quality improvement nurse or the educator. The size of the facility will determine how many of these additional nurses are needed. The Certified Nurse Aide (CNA) is not a licensed nurse, but someone who has been certified by the state to provide nursing or nursing related services.

Employee retention

As mentioned above, the cost to hire an employee is very high. It is worth the effort to retain the good employees that you have rather than constantly hiring and training new employees.

Recently, I did a survey of several long-term care facilities to help determine why employees stay in a particular place.

I asked the following questions:

"What is the most important reason you continue to work in your current location?" The overwhelming answer was comfort in the environment. They liked working there. The second most important reason stated was they liked their co-workers. The third most important reason for staying was that they liked the way their supervisor treated them.

"What do you like most about your job?" Again, there was an overwhelming answer. They said that it was the ability to make a difference for someone else. Benefits, pay, and a great administrator were not nearly as important.

"What would make you leave this facility?" Significant higher wages elsewhere was important. A change of leadership was second.

"What is most important about your relationship with your supervisor?" Respect was the answer.

"Why did you apply at the current community?" Wages was the first answer, followed by reputation of the community and referred by a friend.

Some of these answers surprised me. It is apparent that salary and benefits attract people to one community over another, assuming both provide care to the elderly. What seemed important in keeping employees once they were hired was how they were treated, their relationship with supervisor and co-workers. It comes down to how employees are treated, shown respect, encouraged and rewarded that keeps current employees on board.

There also seems to be something else that attracts and keeps employees that was not mentioned in the survey I conducted. It has to do with pride in your work and pride in your work place. I was associated with a nursing facility that made the newspapers for a high number of deficiencies following an inspection. Shortly after that, we experienced higher turnover of employees than normal. By contrast, a hospital system in the area was ranked as one of the top ten in the nation and began to advertise that they were the employer of choice. They were. It was nearly impossible to get a job with them. They hired only the best people from the large number of applications they received. As a result, their ranking improved until they were ranked as the best hospital system in the country! The point of this illustration is that people have to be proud of where they work and what they do or the social pressure placed upon them will compel them to make a change. Most people seek approval from family, friends and neighbors. If they are providing negative feedback, the result will often times mean that we change what we are doing.

Evaluating

Once employees are hired, it is important to give periodic feedback on how well they are doing. The purpose of this feedback is to correct inappropriate behavior and praise good work. This feedback can be given both informally, with a passing comment or formally, with a ninety-day or annual evaluation. Of the two, the informal evaluation is most effective in making positive changes in work performance.

It is very important when giving feedback to base the feedback on the expectations and how the employee compares with them. If the job description says that the employee will clean the residents rooms each day and the employee cleans only half of the rooms, the feedback should state the expectations, i.e. to have all of the rooms cleaned, and point out that the employee is not meeting it. There may be a good reason why the expectations are not met. By stating the expectations, the employee is informed once again what is expected of them and it offers them an opportunity to explain why they cannot meet the expectations.

Most communities have a three tier progressive disciplinary system in place to deal with employees who cannot or will not abide by company policies. They usually begin with a verbal warning stating that unless the employee makes positive changes, they will lose their job. If the infraction is violated again, a written warning is issued, once again spelling out the results of continued policy infractions. And if for a third time the policy is violated, the employee is normally discharged. This tier system gives the employee amply time to make the changes necessary to keep their position. This should be seen as a helpful system rather than a punitive system.

It is important that the annual and ninety day evaluations be as fair as possible. We are all influenced by a variety of factors as we evaluate those we supervise, but we need to try to look as fairly as possible at the job description compared to the performance. It is good to allow the employee time for feedback on the performance review form. Some reviews ask the employee to evaluate himself or herself while their supervisor does the same. In the end the evaluations are compared and the differences discussed.

Normally, the performance review is the tool that is used to determine if an employee gets a raise and how much. Some companies give everyone a cost of living raise and then allow the employee additional compensation based upon the performance evaluation. Others do not tie the performance to the compensation in any way. The best method seems to be the combination.

Some companies use and ABC or 123 rating for employees as a means of evaluating them. The A or #1 employee is the elite employee who is dedicated to the community and it's mission. He/she can be counted on to perform well in every situation. The B or #2 employee is a solid employee who is a good contributor. This person seldom causes problems and does a steady job day after day. The C or #3 employee is the employee who needs improvement or needs to find another job. Of course, it would be good to have all A employees, but we don't. Recognition, encouragement, promotions and additional responsibility will help keep an A employee in your facility. A progressive discipline policy that is followed will help weed out the C employees. By seeing both the discipline and the encouragement, perhaps the B employees will improve a little as well.

Termination

One of the easiest ways to create problems for your facility is by improperly discharging an employee. Most employees in long-term care facilities are covered under the Social Security Act that makes them eligible for unemployment compensation when they are laid off. Most often, even if the employee has been discharged for policy violations, they may still receive these benefits. Improperly discharging an employee can create discontent with those who remain and can result in legal action and compensation for the discharged employee. Therefore, it is essential that all discharges be done according to your company policies. Most companies follow a simple step process where one infraction results in a verbal warning. The second one results in a written warning. The third offence results in a discharge. There are some offences, like stealing or sleeping on the job, or resident abuse that can result in an immediate discharge. It is essential that you and all the employees understand the policies and imperative that you follow them consistently. Showing favoritism toward an employee you like while enforcing the policies with those you do not like will result in a hearing before the Equal Employment Opportunity Commission.

The best way to avoid the problems of termination and the costs of replacing an employee is to give constant and timely feedback to employees who do not perform according to your facility policies. If someone continues to come in late, a two minute conversation with them about what they will do to correct their behavior lets them know that you know they are late, reinforces the policy that employees are to be at work on time, and gives them an opportunity to correct whatever it is that seems to make them late. If you notice that the behavior has changed, a thirty-second conversation acknowledging the positive change will reinforce the efforts made to correct poor behavior.

Adhering to the policy of praising in public and reprimanding in private will help preserve the integrity of the employee. The result will be happier employees and a smaller turn over ratio. Make time monthly to meet with the employees. Point out some of the good things you have seen them do. Create positive examples for others to follow. Select an employee of the month who best exemplifies your mission or what you expect of an employee. Seek employee and resident nominations for your consideration. These and other recognitions go a long way in retaining good employees and encouraging others to do what is expected.

Employee Records

Each employee should have a record wherein the following information may be found:

Their name, birth date, address, position held in the facility, date employment began, previous employment, social security number, emergency contact name and address, records of formal training received, reference check forms, and date and reason for termination.

They should also have a place that records that they have received the appropriate in-service training as required by the governing agency. Below is an example.

RECORD OF INITIAL STAFF TRAINING
Name_____
Date employed_____
Job Title/Responsibilities:
Training required for all employees dates of training and trainer's initials
Topic:
DateInitials
A. All employees shall be made aware of:
1. The purpose of the facility and service it provides:
2. Required compliance with all regulations as it relates to their duties and responsibilities.
B. All personnel shall be trained in the relevant laws, regulations, and the facility's policies and procedures sufficiently to implement the following:
1. Emergency and disaster plans for the facility;
2. Plans for complying with emergency and disaster plans including evacuating residents when applicable;
3. Use of the first aid kit;
4. Confidential treatment of personal information;
5. Observance of the rights and responsibilities of residents:
6. Procedures for detecting and reporting suspected abuse, neglect or exploitation of residents to the appropriate authorities.
7. Methods for assisting residents in overcoming transfer trauma; and
8. Specific duties and responsibilities of their positions.

_____   _____
Employee signature when above training complete   Date

Additional in-service training should occur that helps the employee either gain new knowledge or relearn something that is important. Nursing home regulations require them for fire safety, abuse, resident rights, infection control, and other fundamental topics that all employees should know. In addition, in-service training should be offered for each new piece of equipment or each new procedure that is introduced. Be sure to record the topic of the in-service, a brief description of what is being communicated by the in-service, the date is was given, who gave it and who attended. Copies of these training event sign in forms should be retained for proof of compliance with regulations.

If an employee is injured on the job, worker's compensation insurance will be used to cover the costs for treatment and lost wages. A record is made of every claim to the insurance company, including the number of days missed and the coast of treatment. The more claims that are made by a particular facility, the higher the cost will be for insurance in the following year. Therefore, it is important to teach the proper techniques for lifting, pushing, pulling, and any other activity that can strain the employee's back. Injuries to the lower back are the most common injury in long-term care facilities. Other typical injuries include needle sticks for nurses, injuries to eyes from chemicals and slipping on wet surfaces. Appropriate precautions can be taken to help employees avoid these injuries. The safety committee should review all injuries and make appropriate recommendations to help avoid similar injuries in the future. The Occupational Safety and Health Act (OSHA) of 1970 was an act that was designed to protect the employee from injury. It has established standards for safety in the work place. An example is that all employees should be able to work in an environment that is free from recognizable hazards that may cause injury or death to an employee. OSHA has the right to inspect the facility at any time for compliance with its regulations and the records of injuries to the employees. This record is to be kept on a form called a Log and Summary of Occupational Injuries and Illnesses. Those injuries recorded on this log are injuries resulting in loss of work, disability or death. The law also requires that the administrator notify the regional, OSHA office within 48 hours of any accidents that cause the deaths of five or more employees. For more information about OSHA consult the district office or consult the Federal Register for a full accounting.

Chapter Fifteen

Maintenance

It is unusual for a long-term care administrator to have a background in maintenance. It is therefore important to be sure that the person you hire to perform this function knows enough about the various systems within the building to keep them functioning. If there is a need for an outside contractor to do work on any of the systems, it would be good if the maintenance coordinator knew enough about the principles of the systems to insure that the work was done adequately.

Knowledge of the various systems will make you a better supervisor. Take the time to learn as much as possible about how the building functions in the event that you need to hire a new maintenance coordinator. Following is a list of things you should know about the building:

Heating and Air conditioning:

What kind of system do you have? Is it a steam system, a hot water system, a forced air system? Are there individual units in each room? How do the systems work? In an emergency, how can you turn off the heat, air or fans? Is there a gas shut off in the event of a fire? Does the system have filters that need to be changed? Are there belts that run equipment that need to be checked each day? What preventive maintenance is required on your system?

Water:

Is there a main water shut off valve? Where is the hot water tank? How does the water get to each room? Are there shut off valves in other locations throughout the facility? Does your system have circulating pumps to pump the hot water to upper floors? Does someone check the water temperature every day?

Fire sprinkler system:

Do you have a wet system that pushes water through the sprinkler heads when the temperature gets to a given point? Do you have a chemical system? What type of system do you have in the kitchen over the range hood? How often are these systems checked? Is a copy sent to the Fire Department code officials?

Call bell system:

How does your call system work? Does the bell need to be reset at the room before it can be used again? Can it be turned off without going to the room to see what the resident needs? How often are they checked? If electricity is lost, how will residents notify the nurse for help? Is the call system on the back up generator?

Fire alarm system:

How is the alarm system monitored? Are the room smoke detectors a part of the fire alarm system? Does your system automatically call both the alarm company and the fire department? Who do you call if there is a trouble light on the fire panel? How does the staff respond to an alarm? Is there a fire plan in place that gives directions for a fire emergency? If not, contact your city Fire Marshall for guidance.

Security:

How does the security system work? What happens when an alarm goes off? Who should respond? Who do you call if there are problems with the system?

Electricity:

Is there a master switch to turn off all the electricity? Where are the breaker panels for certain rooms? How do you reset the tripped circuit? Do you have a generator that backs up the system when you loose electricity? If so, how often is it tested? What does it power? How long can you still function without the power? What emergency plans are in place in the event you must stay in the building and provide limited services to the residents? What emergency plans are in place that determine when you must evacuate the facility?

These are all good questions to ask. Be familiar with the answers so that you can make sure the building continues to function when maintenance personnel are on vacation or ill.

One of the things the maintenance director should do to help insure that the building equipment is working properly is to make regular checks on this equipment. The process of making these regular checks is called a preventive maintenance program. The following is an example of a preventive maintenance schedule.

Equipment	Frequency	Time
Lights	Daily	1 hour
Electric Panels	Daily	30 minutes
Hot Water Readings	Daily	10 minutes
Boiler Room Log	Daily	10 minutes
Cooling Towers	Weekly	30 minutes
Chemicals for Cooling Tower	Weekly	1 hour
Grounds	Weekly	30 minutes
Generator	Weekly	30 minutes
Vehicle Inspection	Bi-weekly	30 minutes
Call Bell System	Monthly	10 minutes per room
Washing Machines and Dryers	Monthly	15 minutes
Handrails	Monthly	30 minutes per floor
Wallpaper	Monthly	30 minutes
Cove Base	Monthly	30 minutes
Personal Protection Equipment	Monthly	1 hour
First Aid Kit	Monthly	10 minutes
Fire Extinguishers	Monthly	1 hour

For each item listed in the above list, there should be a procedure that indicates what needs to be done. Following is an example.

Preventive Maintenance Procedure
Item: Lights
Time required: One Hour
Frequency: Daily
Tools required: None
Materials Used: Light Bulbs
Procedure:
Check all lights in common areas.
Replace burned out lights.
Make work-order for lights needing ballast replacements.
Report any damaged fixtures.

Date	Time	Initials	Date	Time	Initials	Date	Time	Initials

A second form is one where records are kept from recording water temperatures.

Hot Water Temperature Log

Date	Time	Room	Signature	Temperature	Comments

A form like these two should be prepared and kept either at the sight of the equipment or filed in the director's office. Any discrepancies in the norm should alert the maintenance director to a potential problem. Often little problems gone unchecked can end up being larger problems. These can also be used as monitors for the Maintenance CQI program.

The maintenance department should also have some way of being notified when someone else notices a problem or when a project needs to be accomplished. This is often called a work order system. The way the system works is that a form is completed indicating what needs to be done. The maintenance coordinator picks up the form and prioritizes what should be done when and by whom. After the work is complete, a follow up phone call to the person submitting the request to see if the work was completed to their satisfaction. The following is an example of a work order form.

Matienance Work/Repair Request Worksheet

Unit\Locattion:_____

Date of request:_____Name of person making request:_____

Phone #:_____

Description of request:_____

Work preformed:

Completed by:_____Date:_____

As the administrator, is it important that you understand the Life Safety Code. It determines a great deal about the building as it applies to the safety of the residents and staff. Following is a brief overview of the code. Purchase a copy of it to understand completely what is required of your facility.

LIFE SAFETY CODE CHECKLIST

Department Fire Plan and Evacuation Map

Your facility must establish a narrative fire plan that includes the actions to be taken in case of fire. There should be a fire evacuation map in each hallway that includes:

A sketch of all rooms in the zone.

A marking that shows, you are here.

Red arrows showing the primary evacuation route and yellow arrows showing the secondary route.

The identity of exterior exits for each route.

Monthly inspection of fire extinguishers.

All extinguishers should be serviced insuring that hoses are not cracked, nozzles obstructed, or seal broken.

The pressure gauge on each extinguisher should be in the operable range.

There should be a Fire Extinguisher Inspection Record available on each extinguisher.

All extinguishers should be checked every month and initialed

Electrical Systems

All electrical cords should be in serviceable condition.

No extension cords should be used by residents or the facility.

All coffee makers should be placed on a nonflammable surface, with a safety check on the machine to insure that it shuts off after a certain period of time.

No inappropriate adapters should be used on electrical plugs.

All personal electrical devices should be inspected and a safety sticker with inspector's initials and date should be placed on them.

D. *Flammable/Combustible Liquids and Gases*

All compressed gas cylinders (oxygen, carbon dioxide, nitrous oxide, etc.) must be chained (secured) so as to prevent falling.

Any flammable storage cabinets should be marked: "FLAMMABLE MATERIAL."

All compressed gas cylinders, not in use, must have a cylinder cap.

All staff members should know the location of oxygen shut-off valves.

E. *Exits*

No fire doors should be propped open.

All exits should be clearly marked, illuminated and operational.

All exits should be easily opened.

All hold-open mechanisms should be in working order and all doors close entirely when tested.

All corridors or passageways required for exit access must have at least a 44 inch clear travel path.

All smoke barrier doors (metal double doors in main passageways) must have a gap of less than four inches when closed.

Nothing should block fire exit doors from the outside or the inside.

F. *Resident and Staff Safety.*

All poisonous materials must be stored in locked cabinet with antidote information displayed.

All sharps should be discarded in prescribed containers and the containers should be discarded when over ¾ full.

All precautions should be taken to insure that floors are clean and clear.

All wastebaskets should be constructed of nonflammable material.

All biohazard waste, including sharps, should be disposed of in the proper receptacle.

Nothing should be stored in stairwells.

No portable heaters should be used in the facility.

All storage areas should be neat and clean.

All ceiling tiles should be in place without any visible stains.

Material may not be stored closer than 18 inches from the ceiling in sprinkled areas.

All new employees must be in-serviced on the hazards of their job and this in-service must be documented.

Eating and drinking should be prohibited where toxic or infectious wastes are routinely present.

Personal protective equipment should be provided and utilized by personnel working with or around hazardous materials including body fluids.

Hazardous Materials

If flammable vapors are present, take precautions to prevent ignition by eliminating or controlling the sources of ignition. All containers should be in good shape with no cracks or broken parts. A copy of a recent AUL should be on file. All the items in the cabinets should match the AUL. None of the items in the lockers should have expired shelf life date. Not more than 5 gallons of Class I or II liquids or 10 gallons of Class III liquids should be stored in a storage unit. No containers of hazardous materials should be stored outside the locker.

Spills Procedures

Spill procedures should be located in the work area.

All personnel should be competent in knowing and demonstrating spill procedures.

All personnel should be knowledgeable in disposal procedures.

Resident safety is very important. Develop policies and procedures to insure that the Life Safety Code is being followed. The long-term care community facility should also develop a plan for the protection of both the residents and the facility in the event of a fire. The plan should identify step by step what should be done if a smoke detector goes off, if a fire alarm sounds or if smoke is detected. Each month on alternating shifts, a fire drill should be conducted that trains both the residents and the staff in appropriate response to different scenarios. There should be a drawing displayed on each floor showing alternate exits, telephones, fire alarm boxes, and fire extinguishers.

The telephone number for the fire department, rescue and police should be posted on each phone shown on the drawing. These are usually in the nurses' station. All staff members should be fully aware of the fire plan, their responsibilities, the location of fire extinguishers and fire alarm boxes or pull stations.

The approved fire plan should be reviewed quarterly with all residents and staff.

Fire drills shall be held each month for the staff on duty and all residents. During the three-month period, at least one drill should be held during each shift and all should be unannounced. Following each fire drill, an evaluation should occur to determine how well the staff and residents have complied with the drill.

Below is an example of a fire plan.

In the event of a fire or fire drill, keep calm; DO NOT PANIC. Reassure residents and maintain a calm atmosphere. Follow immediately the basic steps of RACE as outlined below.

RACE AGAINST FIRE

R: RESCUE, Remove resident(s) from danger. Close door behind you.

A: ALARM, Pull the nearest fire alarm, CALL 911. Execute your fire emergency plan.

C: CONFINE, Close resident room doors and windows. The decision to evacuate the facility is made ONLY by the Fire Marshall or the director. Ask visitors to remain with the residents.

E: EXTINGUISH, Extinguish only small contained fires, i.e. Trashcan, etc.

*NEVER EVACUATE UNTIL THE FIRE EVACUATION ORDER HAS BEEN GIVEN BY THE FIRE DEPARTMENT OR THE DIRECTOR.

*BE READY FOR ANY EMERGENCY.

General Fire Safety Information For All Employees

If you discover fire:
1. Remove residents from the scene of fire or smoke.
2. Sound alarm, CALL 911
3. Close doors and windows
4. Get behind a closed door

The "ALL CLEAR" signal will be given by the director of maintenance or the nursing supervisor

When the alarm rings:
1.Close all windows and doors. Leave doors unlocked.
2. Do not use a fire extinguisher on a person.
3. Remain in your assigned area until given further instructions.
4. Never leave your post until all residents are in safe areas.

SEE DEPARTMENTAL LISTINGS BELOW FOR SPECIFIC INSTRUC-TIONS.

EMPLOYEE RESPONSIBILITIES:

The administrator, or designee, has overall responsibility for the facility and will be the Fire Department contact. Decisions for media announcements, if needed, will only be approved by the administrator.

CHAIN OF COMMAND:

In the absence of the administrator, the director of nursing or the assistant director of nursing will coordinate staff and residents. In the absence of all of these administrative staff, the nursing supervisor will assume responsibility of decision making until relieved by the Fire Department.

RECEPTIONIST:

1. Call Fire Department. Dial 911.

2. Notify maintenance by way of the walkie-talkie.

3. Outside callers will be informed that calls cannot be taken. Example: "We need to leave the switchboard clear in case of emergency calls."

SECRETARY:

The Secretary, Administrative office staff will report to the main dining room to receive all communications.

A. DEPARTMENTAL RESPONSIBILITIES:

Nursing:

1. Move residents behind the nearest closed door.

2. Be sure all windows and doors are closed.

3. Stay at nurses' station for further instructions.

B. BEAUTY SHOP:

Beauty Shop personnel and residents and Lemon Tree personnel and residents will remain in their respective rooms with the door closed.

C. BUSINESS OFFICE:

Business office personnel will secure all records and equipment. Leave door unlocked and report to the main Dining room to assist as directed.

D. HOUSEKEEPING:

Housekeeping personnel cleaning apartments will leave the rooms, close the doors and leave them unlocked. They will take their carts to the nearest common area, being sure they are clear of all passage areas. Housekeepers on the floor where fire is located will go to the solarium or lounge furthest from the scene of the fire. Housekeepers will wait in the common areas for further instructions or until an "ALL CLEAR" is announced.

E. FOOD SERVICE:

Exhaust fans and all appliances will be shut off.

All Food Service employees will report to the dining room when the alarm sounds and assist as directed. All residents and guests will remain in the dining room until an "ALL CLEAR" is announced.

F. MAINTENANCE:

When the alarm sounds, or notification is received, maintenance personnel will report to the lobby to verify location of fire and then use radio to report location to nursing supervisor. Each person is to carry a fire extinguisher with him/her to the location of the fire. There is an ABC dry chemical extinguisher on each floor. Move endangered person(s) from the room/immediate area of the fire. The director of maintenance or his/her assistant will assign his/her personnel to specific duties, either at the scene of the fire or in other areas of the building. Ventilation and electrical equipment shut down will be carried out as per Fire Department instructions.

The director of maintenance will be responsible for conducting monthly fire drills (alternating the shift 7-3, 3-11, 11-7) and give the "ALL CLEAR" signal at the end of the drill.

G. RESIDENT ACTIVITIES:

Resident activities coordinator will report to the main dining room and assist as needed.

This example shows how important it is to be prepared. Each month a fire drill should be conducted using a variety of scenarios so that the staff and the residents will respond appropriately. Many states require that a record be kept of these fire drills. It is best to check with the licensing agency to see what is required before creating a form of your own. The following is an example of what is required in the state of Virginia.

RECORD OF MONTHLY AND OTHER REQUIRED FIRE DRILLS
DATE:
TIME
NUMBER OF STAFF PARTICIPATING:
NUMBER OF RESIDENT PARTICIPATING:
TIME REQUIRED TO PRACTICE APPROVED FIRE PLAN:

The drills should include sounding the alarms, building evacuation, if the plan requires it, timing the drill, practice in alerting fire authorities, simulated use of fire fighting equipment, practice of fire containment procedures, and any other procedure as required by the plan.

Many states require inspections annually. The most common is the Fire Marshall inspection. Remaining compliant with life safety codes and local fire department regulations will help insure resident safety.

It is no secret that smoke kills more people than fire. Develop smoking regulations and operate within them. There should be no smoking allowed in the residents rooms or in any area deemed to be hazardous. If a special section of the facility is designated as a smoking area be sure there is nothing in the area that could catch fire. Ashtrays and waste paper baskets should be metal to prevent any chance of a fire. If a resident is irresponsible due to a mental condition, a staff member or volunteer must assist them and remain with them when they smoke.

It makes sense to only purchase furnishings for a room that are flame resistant. Bedding and curtains seem to be the things that catch fire when a resident is non-compliant with the smoking regulations. Be sure that doors that are on a self closer are able to do so. They are self closing to keep out smoke and fire in an effort to safe lives. By allowing self-closing doors to be propped open, the fire safety system built into the facility is bypassed and the result could be death, law suite or a citation by the local Fire Marshall.

Most nursing homes are built so that a fire can be easily extinguished using a defend in place method. That is why it is important to rescue the resident and close the door so that the sprinkler system can extinguish the fire. Many of the newer assisted living facilities also have sprinkler systems but are of wooden construction. Because a facility is wooden and not block construction, there will be considerations on evacuation of residents that the Fire Marshall will make plain when a certificate of occupancy is granted or during annual inspections. Multiple story buildings of wooden construction are of particular concern to firemen. Firewalls with a two hour fire resistance are required in these structures.

Emergency procedures:

The facility should also have on hand procedures for emergencies, including severe weather, loss of utilities, missing persons, and severe injury. These emergency plans and the fire plan should be discussed at orientation, with new residents, and with volunteers.

Emergency calls:

All long-term care facilities should have a call system available for residents to call for help. The staff should be able to determine what room has called for help. If this does not happen, staff will make rounds at least once per hour to monitor for emergencies while residents are asleep.

The following is a summary of regulations that are typical of what would be appropriate for assisted living facilities regarding facility maintenance.

All doors close readily and efficiently. This is especially true of fire doors. Fire doors that are held open by a magnetic device should close freely and completely. Any door that has a self closer on it should only be held open with a magnetic device that is tied into the fire alarm system.

Doors or windows used for ventilation should be screened.

There shall be enclosed walkways between resident rooms and dining and sitting areas that are adequately lighted, heated and ventilated. If a facility has more than one section and residents are required to move from one section to another, the enclosure is required.

There shall be an ample supply of hot and cold water at all times. The hot water should range between 105 and 120 degrees Fahrenheit coming from the resident's tap. Taking a temperature reading each day, as a part of a preventive maintenance program, will insure that the water is not too hot so as to harm the resident. Many of the whirlpool tubs available have their own control value that will alarm if the incoming water exceeds a given limit.

The interior and exterior of all buildings shall be maintained in good order, free of rubbish and free of foul, stale or musty odors. Odors are an indication of a problem. Exterior checks for potential problems will identify the problems before they become odors.

Grounds should be properly maintained, including mowing of grass and removal of snow and ice. Each facility should be aware of the risks of fall, especially in the winter months. It is the responsibility of the maintenance department to use whatever materials and procedures necessary to prevent residents or staff members from falling.

Adequate provisions shall be made for disposal of garbage in covered, vermin-proof, watertight containers that are emptied and cleaned once per week. Simply making sure the lids and doors to dumpsters are closed at all times will help control pests and odor. Trash that spills out of the container attracts rats, flies and numerous other pests.

The buildings shall be kept free of flies, roaches, ants and other vermin and the grounds free of their breeding places. Contracting with a company to inspect and treat the facility will help prevent these pests from becoming a health problem. Keeping the building clean and dry will also be helpful.

All furnishings shall be kept clean and in good repair.

Steps shall have a nonskid surface.

Elevator shall be inspected annually and certificate of the same available.

Heat shall be supplied from a central heating system or approved electrical system. When outside temperature are below 65, the inside temperatures should be at least 72. Neither the facility nor the residents should use portable heating devices. When inside temperatures exceed 85, cooling devices shall be made available to residents. Electrical fans must be screened and placed for the protection of the residents.

All areas of the facility shall be well lighted to provide safety and comfort for residents. This is also true for outside parking lots, hallways, stairwells, foyers, doorways and exits.

Resident sleeping areas should follow the national BOCA codes and provide at least 450 cubic feet of air space per person. There should be at least 100 square feet of floor space in bedrooms accommodating a resident and ceiling should be at least seven and one have feet high. At least one window measuring eight square feet should be available for each resident in a room. For semi-private rooms, the window space should measure at least six square feet per person. The rooms should allow for at least three feet of space between beds if they are used as a semi-private. No bedroom shall be used as a corridor to any other room.

Bathrooms equipped to accommodate more than one person at a time shall be labeled by sex and provide visual privacy and ventilation.

Handrails are to be available near bathtubs, grab bars by toilets and stools by shower stalls.

These codes are similar to those established for nursing facilities. If the administrator knows the codes and shares this knowledge with the director of maintenance, then when the inspectors come to visit, they should find no problems with the building and grounds. The section of the Code of Federal Regulations that pertains to maintenance provides is 483.70 and it says:

"The facility must be designed, constructed, equipped, and maintained to protect the health and safety of residents, personnel and the public.

The facility must meet the applicable provisions of the 2000 edition of the Life Safety Code of the National Fire Protection Association.

The facility must be in compliance with Chapter 19.2.9, Emergency Lighting.

An emergency electrical power system must supply power adequate at least for lighting all entrances and exits; equipment to maintain the fire detection, alarm, and extinguishing systems; and life support systems in the event the normal electrical supply is interrupted.

When life support systems are used, the facility must provide emergency electrical power with an emergency generator (as defined in NFPA 99, Health Care Facilities) that is located on the premises.

The facility must provide sufficient space and equipment in dining, health services, recreation, and program areas to enable staff to provide residents with needed services as required by these standards and as identified in each resident's plan of care; and maintain all essential mechanical, electrical, and patient care equipment in safe operating condition.

Resident rooms must be designed and equipped for adequate nursing care, comfort, and privacy of residents.

(1) Bedrooms must:

(i) Accommodate no more than four residents;

(ii) Measure at least 80 square feet per resident in multiple resident bedrooms, and at least 100 square feet in single resident rooms;

(iii) Have direct access to an exit corridor;

(iv) Be designed or equipped to assure full visual privacy for each resident;

(v) In facilities initially certified after March 31, 1992, except in private rooms, each bed must have ceiling suspended curtains, which extend around the bed to provide total visual privacy in combination with adjacent walls and curtains;

(vi) Have at least one window to the outside; and

(vii) Have a floor at or above grade level.

(2) The facility must provide each resident with:

(i) A separate bed of proper size and height for the convenience of the resident;

(ii) A clean, comfortable mattress;

(iii) Bedding appropriate to the weather and climate; and

(iv) Functional furniture appropriate to the resident's needs, and individual closet space in the resident's bedroom with clothes racks and shelves accessible to the resident.

Each resident room must be equipped with or located near toilet and bathing facilities.

The nurse's station must be equipped to receive resident calls through a communication system from:

(1) Resident rooms; and

(2) Toilet and bathing facilities.

The facility must provide one or more rooms designated for resident dining and activities. These rooms must:

(1) Be well lighted;

(2) Be well ventilated, with nonsmoking areas identified;

(3) Be adequately furnished; and

(4) Have sufficient space to accommodate all activities.

The facility must provide a safe, functional, sanitary, and comfortable environment for the residents, staff and the public. The facility must:

(1) Establish procedures to ensure that water is available to essential areas when there is a loss of normal water supply;

(2) Have adequate outside ventilation by means of windows, or mechanical ventilation, or a combination of the two;

(3) Equip corridors with firmly secured handrails on each side; and

(4) Maintain an effective pest control program so that the facility is free of pests and rodents."[26]

Dining and resident activities spaces.

The facility must provide one or more rooms designated for resident dining and activities. These rooms must:

(1) Be well lighted;

(2) Be well ventilated, with nonsmoking areas identified;

(3) Be adequately furnished; and

(4) Have sufficient space to accommodate all activities.

The facility must provide a safe, functional, sanitary, and comfortable environment for the residents, staff and the public. The facility must:

(1) Establish procedures to ensure that water is available to essential areas when there is a loss of normal water supply;

(2) Have adequate outside ventilation by means of windows, or mechanical ventilation, or a combination of the two;

(3) Equip corridors with firmly secured handrails on each side; and

(4) Maintain an effective pest control program so that the facility is free of pests and rodents.[27]

Chapter Sixteen

Marketing

Marketing is an essential part of the future growth of any long-term care facility. Many times, in the assisted living facilities or smaller nursing homes, the administrator is asked to perform this function or assist in it, therefore, it is important that he/she understand the basics of marketing. In nursing homes or continuing care retirement communities, the administrator may be pressed to give a tour or talk to a special family.

Sales

Marketing begins with sales. Even though the rooms are rented in most long-term care communities, the term *sales* applies to rentals as well. Selling the facility to a potential resident requires that the person doing the selling knows their product. It is essential that the sales person understand what he/she has to offer compared to the competition. Visiting the competitor is important. Comparing facilities will help the marketing staff better understand the product being offered by other communities and how they compare with what they offer. It is also important that the potential buyers know exactly what the long-term care facility has to offer. There should be a written program description available to prospective residents that describes the people to be served, the license the facility holds and any limits to the care provided. This tells prospective residents very clearly what they can expect from a particular facility.

Good listening habits are essential to sales. It is important that anyone who is trying to sell begin by listening to the needs of the person who is inquiring. The person doing the marketing must do their best to put the other person at ease. It is essential that the marketing person understand the needs of the person inquiring. They must focus on the person talking, pay attention to what they are saying, and take notes as they talk to serve as a reminder of what is important to them. When the potential resident has finished saying what they are looking for or why they have come to the facility, it is time to ask questions for clarification. The only time it is appropriate to interrupt the inquiring person is if it is clear they have come to the wrong kind of facility. Perhaps the person needs skilled nursing care or they indicate that they have qualified for Medicaid and your facility does not accept Medicaid. In these cases the marketing person should explain their concern and ask for clarification from them to make sure the person could not possibly come have their needs met at the community. If not, by knowing the competition, the marketing person could make an appropriate recommendation.

Avoid doing things like interrupting, correcting grammar, finishing the speaker's sentences, answering the phone or appearing inpatient. Attention should be paid to what the person is saying in order to be prepared to sell to meet their need. The chances for increasing sales are directly related to the degree of enthusiasm the sales person is able to develop in their facility. Positive emotions about a product don't come from product knowledge or selling skills but from our own personal experiences with what is being sold. Commitment to what is being sold will encourage the prospective resident to make a financial commitment to the community. The marketing person should use positive, upbeat examples of how needs were met in other situations to help convince the prospective resident that the staff could do the same for them.

Potential customers often times make decisions based upon first impressions. Here are some ways to make a good fist impression:

1. Pay attention to the prospect. Sit across from them and make eye contact.

2. Make them feel comfortable. Offer some refreshments.

3. Ask what you can do for them and listen to what they tell you.

4. Smile and be reassuring. Visiting a long-term care community can be difficult emotionally.

5. Use the other person's name often. Sales are based more on impressions than reality.

Inquiries

Inquiries are people who inquire about your community or your services. Inquiries will come to the community by telephone calls, when people simply walk in, by mail, and through the website. The telephone is by far the most common type of inquiry. It creates a first impression and provides an opportunity to learn about the prospect. The walk in is the second most common type of inquiry. When someone comes to the building, it creates a lasting impression and provides an opportunity to relate in person. The third kind of inquire is the mail. This type of inquiry usually reflects an interest for sometime down the road, but that is not always the case. It also provides an opportunity to follow-up. Often times the mail inquiries are as a result of a direct mail campaign. The fourth type of inquiry is the website visit. If information is requested, then this provides an opportunity for follow up, otherwise it can be seen as advertising that may generate an inquire.

I. Telephone Inquiries

As discussed earlier, most prospects will inquire by telephone. The telephone inquiry will create the prospect's first impression of the community. Make sure the staff uses their best telephone etiquette skills. Telephone etiquette is also the key to beginning a strong rapport with prospects. When someone contacts the community by phone, the person who answers the phone is taking the first step in building a relationship. The initial phone call is the first opportunity to make a good first impression, gather important information and begin qualifying the prospect. Potential residents may be lost within the first few minutes of telephone contact simply because the call was not handled properly. During a telephone inquiry, prospects are sensitive to the way they are treated. They will listen to background noise, interruptions and the politeness (or lack of politeness) shown to them. The prospect will make a judgment of the community based on what they heard, the accent of the person answering the phone, how quickly the phone is answered and how long they are placed on hold before getting to someone who can answer their questions. Their judgment will translate to an assessment of the care the community provides.

Encourage the receptionist to answer the phone within three rings and to identify the community and themselves. They should speak clearly and slowly. Non-verbal cues are important; therefore, it is important to greet the caller with a friendly, upbeat voice. Always keep a form by the telephone so that whoever answers it will be able to record the caller's name and check for accurate spelling. Be sure the receptionist asks the caller how he/she heard about the community. This information helps to identify which marketing or networking efforts is working best. Have them take notes. Do not allow the receptionist to hang up before recording the caller's address and phone number. Follow up information cannot be provided without them.

People call for three reasons: to buy, to gain information so they can eliminate the facility, and to avoid involvement. There is sufficient interest or motivation to pick up the phone. These are good prospects if they are developed early. There is so much competition out there, so many different options; everybody wants a reason to narrow their choices. They will look for any excuse to cross a facility off their list so that they are not so overwhelmed. They have a fear of intimidation and the hard sell. The phone is less threatening. Be sure to respond quickly to any phone inquiries.

II. Mail Inquiries

Occasionally, a prospect will hear about a community and take the time to send a hand-written note. Most mail inquires are the result of an advertisement or similar kind of promotion. As discussed earlier, mail inquiries are the least common type of inquiry. The mail inquiry usually reflects a future interest and/or a request for information. If a prospect corresponds in writing, he/she has more than likely requested information from several of your competitors as well. Be sure that your reply stands out from other replies the inquirer may be receiving. Respond immediately to all mail inquiries with a phone call. All inquiries are valuable. Take written inquiries seriously. The sooner the relationship moves to a phone contact, the better. When calling, introduce yourself and explain to the prospect that you are following you on their inquiry. Gently try to determine why the prospect has contacted you. Gather as much information as you can. Invite the prospect to visit the community.

III. Electronic Mail

Facilities that offer websites often get requests for more information from that website. Many times other websites offer links to the facility website and once again, a request can be made while surfing the web. Although most potential residents are in the eighties and are therefore not very comfortable using the computer and conducting web searches, their children and grandchildren are. When an inquire comes via e-mail, treat it formally, as if it were a written letter. Respond to it with a phone call if possible, but if not in writing on letterhead with the expressed goal of inviting the potential resident to visit the community. If no address is given beyond an e-mail address, design a format that looks as much like a formal letter as possible and respond as soon as possible.

IV. Walk in's

Occasionally, prospective residents or family members will come to the facility without calling or having any information about it. They may be aware the facility is there because they live in the area or drive by it on the way to work. These folks are called walk-ins because they do just that. Sometimes appointments are made, but more often than not, they just stop by to inquire. The person who comes to visit the facility with or without an appointment will be looking very closely at the facility from the moment they enter the property. The adage about curb appeal for houses is true also for long-term care communities. The sign out front, the length of the grass, the paint on the curb, and the distance to the front door all make an impression. Once inside, the prospects will carefully inspect the physical aspects of the community. Small messes, untidy areas, or an overall lack of cleanliness are red flags for most prospects. After all, if the community's carpets are not clean, then how can the facility be trusted to care for the prospect's loved one? The small details create powerful impressions. Prospects remember most clearly what they did NOT like about your community. After all, they may be visiting several and need to determine those that do not meet their needs or standards.

If a prospect calls in or comes into the community, the following interview techniques will be helpful.

Develop a special place to sit and interview. It can be a library, chapel or lounge. Try not to use an office. Make the setting comfortable and private.

Clear your mind and listen. Focus in on what they are saying.

Take notes to help you remember questions you may want to come back to when they finish talking.

Use non-direct questions at first to allow the prospect to continue to go where he/she will in the interview.

Encourage them to tell their story from the beginning to the end.

Identify all of the important decision makers in the family. Write their names down.

If necessary, ask for more detail.

Try to determine when they may be interested in moving in.

Ask direct questions of clarification

Summarize what you have heard and seek affirmation.

Tours

Once a person visits the facility, the marketing staff member should be ready to give a presentation to them. This is the opportunity to listen and then sell to meet the needs of the potential buyer. Here is a suggested outline for making a presentation.

Tours should follow the sit-tour-sit format. The moment a potential resident or family member enters the facility, they are making decisions about it, by what they observe. The marketing staff member should take the time to build a relationship with them and discover their concerns. The interviewing techniques listed above will help do this. During this time, while listening and taking notes, the sales person must be asking themselves some basic qualifying questions so that they do not waste their time or the time of the person inquiring.

1. Can your community meet the resident's needs?

The sales person will eventually look at the entire scope of needs: medical, social, and personal. The priority should be to focus on medical needs. The community's ability to meet the resident's medical needs is clearly a qualifying factor. Often families will contact an assisted living community assuming they are a nursing home or they may go to a nursing facility and need only the services offered in an assisted living community. Explaining up front what services are and are not provided will help to quickly qualify potential residents. Some states require that printed information be sent to prospective residents explaining the services provided so there is no misunderstanding.

2. Can the prospective resident afford your community?

The prospect will be qualified based on his/her ability to afford your services. If the services are cost prohibitive, there is no reason to continue with the sales process. Most often prospects, especially children of prospects, will ask for prices very early on in the process. It may be the first question they ask when they call. This should be an indication that money is a concern to them.

3. What is the urgency of placement?

The final step in qualifying is to determine the prospect's time frame. Do not rule out a prospect due to her intended time frame. Knowing the time frame for admission will help prioritize follow-up and ongoing interactions with the potential resident. In other words, the resident who is going to move in within three months is a higher priority than the one who does not plan to move in for six months or longer.

Once the marketing staff member understands the answers to these questions, it is important to ask questions that help them understand what is important to the prospective residents. These may be questions like what their interests are and what they are looking for in a long-term care facility. Once the marketing person has determined what is important to the potential resident, then it is time to take them on a tour of the building; emphasizing how the facility can match their needs.

The tour should be based on the needs and interests expressed by the potential resident. If activities are important, show them that area. If rehab is necessary, show them the therapy areas.

During the tour, show the model apartment. Open the door and let the prospective resident or family members wander where they choose. This will indicate areas of importance to them. Answer any questions they may have and point out pertinent features (call lights, etc.) if necessary. Only show an inhabited room with permission. Families will respect this.

Most prospects will need services within six months. However, long-range planners may not require the services offered by the facility for several years. Nursing homes and assisted living facilities are often times facilities that are selected based on an immediate need; a family member is ill or hospitalized. Continuing care retirement communities that offer independent living apartments are examples of places where a couple or family may begin to look around in advance of an immediate need.

Prioritize and manage the time available for marketing so that the time schedule of the prospect is taken into consideration.

The effectiveness of the tour will, in all likelihood, make or break the sale. Prospects of all personality types see, hear, taste, and touch what the facility has to offer. What they experience is what they use to make their decision. During a tour, the prospect assesses what it would feel like to live in the community or how he/she would feel about placing a parent there.

Fifteen minutes prior to each scheduled tour do a quick check up on all areas of the community that are normally highlighted during the tour. Although this takes a little extra effort, it is well worth it in the long run. By troubleshooting before the tour, it is possible to eliminate interruptions and poor impressions during the tour. Let the staff know you have a tour coming and avoid areas that create a negative impression.

Never use a standard tour. Instead, customize the tour to address the unique needs of the individual prospect. The way the marketing person treats the residents staff and potential resident while on the tour will answer one of the prospects most important questions. "Will they treat me or my parent well?" When giving a tour of the community, strive to try to preserve the dignity and protect the privacy of every resident. If a resident's room is to be shown, get permission from the resident before entering. Make sure the prospect knows permission has been given, and knock before entering.

Once the tour is complete, the person giving the tour should take the prospect to a comfortable, private place to get their reactions to the tour and answer any questions they may have. They should be alert for and buying signals such as "Oh, this is nice. Mom would like it here." It is very important to ask for either a commitment or a deposit of some sort after hearing these kinds of positive comments. Closing the sale is helping the prospect make a decision to select your community. It is the moment of truth. All that has been done prior to this point has helped get to this point. Closing a sale is not just about the ability to ask for the deposit at the very end of the process, but the sales person's ability throughout the process. The sales person must ask him/herself if they gathered information during the inquiry stage, actively listened to what the prospective has been telling him/her, appropriately qualified the prospect, presented the benefits of the community and effectively handled objections. If each step in the sales process is handled effectively, the close will come very easily.

If the prospect or family member is not yet ready to make a deposit, then the marketing staff member should initiate the next step. This may be setting up a follow-up tour or deciding when would be a good time to make a follow up phone call in a few days to see how they are doing in the decision making. Escort them to the door. (Remember, the tour is not done until the family has left the parking lot.) Immediately take care of any paperwork or follow-up details. Send a handwritten thank you note within three days of the tour.

The following reports were done using a data base program. The advantage of such computerized programs is that the computer will perform the calculations each week. They are reports that are important for tracking activity as well as responses.

Weekly Marketing Sales Report Inquire Activity
# of new inquires from total inquires

Date	E-mail	Phone	Mail	Website	Walk in	Event		Initial	Repeat
Total									

This form enables you to track all inquires to determine if your marketing plan is working or to give you information on where you need to increase funding for a particular means of attracting residents.

Weekly Marketing Inquire Report Inquire Information
Why inquired:
Who inquired:

Date	Future need	Immediate need		Self	Family member	Friend	Professional

This chart shows who inquired and why. Again, this information will help you plan your marketing for the future.

Weekly Marketing Referral Report
How did the inquirer hear about us?

Date	Ad	Church	Web site	Direct mail	Friend	Professional	Phone book	Knows area	Radio/TV	Other
Total										

This chart also tells you where to spend your money or who to thank for a referral.

Weekly Marketing Results Report
Result of inquire
Inquire disqualified for:

Date	Sent brochure	Sent packet	Apt. made		Financial reasons	Medical reasons	Other

This form lets you know what has happened as a result of an inquire. Each inquire from the previous charts should have a result identified here.

Weekly Marketing Appointment Report
Deposits
Apt. Type:
Received:
Tour Survey Results:

Date	Studio	One bedroom	10%	# Sent out	# Returned	# Still interested	# Not interested
Total							

This chart provides a quick view of what kind of rooms are selling along with the results of a post tour survey.

Weekly Marketing Potential Resident Report
Application complete and deposits made
Within 30 days Within 60 days Within 90 days Total

Date	Studio	One bedroom		Studio	One bedroom		Studio	One bedroom			

This chart lets you know what move in activity is projected for the future.

Effective Management of Inquiries

Not everyone who comes in for a tour will be ready to make a deposit that day or to make a decision that day. It is therefore very important that the Marketing person keep track of those who have inquired by any means. Once a sufficient number of inquiries and referrals have been generated, they must be managed effectively. Doing so will help convert inquiries (both leads and referrals) into tours, and convert tours into sales. Calling referral sources for appointments is the first step in generating inquiries. Using the inquire management system is the second. Regardless of what system is used, it is important to track and plan the visits and to record the comments written after the visits. Plan to spend nearly 50 percent of your time on the phone. Ideally, the phone will be ringing frequently. People who have heard about the community or have seen the ads will be calling to inquire. Phone calls will also come from professional networking contacts that are making referrals and from prospects that will inquire after seeing advertisements, attending an event at the community, receiving a direct mail piece or reading an article about the community.

Networking

Networking is a strategy used for building ongoing, mutually beneficial relationships. Most often the administrator or the marketing staff will network with professionals in the local community and with resident's family members. Networking is about building lasting relationships. Effective networking will produce relationships that become mutually beneficial for all those involved. However, as with relationships of any kind, networking relationships require time and attention.

Networking and advertising working together

Advertising increases awareness and reaches many people at one time. It is possible to use advertising and networking together to achieve the marketing goals. But networking still generates *more qualified referrals that have immediate needs.*

Networking with Professionals

There are dozens of opportunities for networking in the facility. Here is a list of potential referral sources to consider. Those listed in the left column are those who typically have clients with more immediate needs for assisted living or nursing home services.

Immediate referrals	Other Referral Sources
Hospital Social Workers/Discharge Planners	Referral Agencies
Family Practice Physicians	Case Managers
Geriatric Physicians	Human Service Agency Social Workers
Orthopedic Physicians	Worship Centers
Podiatrists	Senior Citizen Organizations
Independent Living Communities	Employee Assistance Program Counselors
Adult Day Care Centers	Realtors -Relocation Specialists
Elder Care Attorneys	Organizations
Trust Officers Managed Care	Local Human Resource Departments
Your "competition"-Nursing Homes, Home Health Agencies, Adult Day Care	Pharmacists

Satisfied family members of current residents are an ideal group of people to network because they already understand your product and services, they are satisfied and speak well of your community and they generally know other people who are looking for long-term care options. A successful networking relationship is one where the marketing person or the administrator and the contact can meet each other's needs and where the relationship shared has a foundation of trust. If neither person can meet the other's needs, there is no reason for a relationship. The facility needs quality referrals from this new relationship. It is important that the referral understands this. Before beginning the relationship, the marketing staff member should determine if the referral could offer what the facility needs. Once that is clarified, determine what they need. Most often it is a safe and supportive healthcare environment offering quality care for their clients. Discharge planners are under pressure to discharge patients from their hospitals. Their goal is to find appropriate care environments for patients in a timely manner. Their needs can be met by being available, responding quickly, and accepting move-ins within 24-hours. Establishing strong relationships with local discharge planners is very important. Some physicians have patients with a variety of long-term care needs. This makes physicians a great networking resource. They can meet the facilities needs by referring their patients. Physicians want their patients in settings where quality care is the priority. They are also interested in growing their practices. The facility can help meet physicians needs by providing quality care for their patients and by referring residents who do not have physicians to these referral sources. A primary reason referral sources want to build a relationship with a facility is to make their job easier. The marketing staff and the administrator must learn to satisfy their needs and help them solve their problems. Failing to do so may mean that these sources will no longer refer to the facility. Trust is key to any relationship. It is a key in selling the community to leads and it is also true in the professional networking relationships. Building trust is another investment of the marketing person's time. They need to get to know the referral source, to keep in touch with them and prove that they are trustworthy. Building trust comes by developing rapport and satisfying the referral's needs. The best way to build rapport is to meet the referral on a regular basis. Doing this will enable the marketing staff member to remain up-to-date on the referrals, and to keep them up-to-date on the needs of the community, and to be able to ask for referrals face to face. Networking efforts do require time. But when properly planned, networking will become a comfortable part of your routine. Relationships require the marketing staff members an occasionally the administrator to be involved.

The following table illustrates the recommended number of priority contacts.

Number of Apartments in the community	Number of priority A contacts	Number of Good B and C contracts
50	8	16
60	10	20
70	12	24
80	14	28
90	16	32
100	18	36
110	19	38
120	20	40
200	34	68

A networking meeting is a face-to-face visit between you and your contact.

During every face-to-face meeting, the marketing staff person should try to re-establish rapport, clarify the contact's needs, communicate relevant information about the facility and ask the contact how well they are meeting his/her needs. Seek feedback on the care that the facility is providing and correct any misperceptions.

Frequency

The frequency of the referral meetings is related to the ABC priority that was discussed earlier in this chapter. The higher the priority, the more often it is necessary to meet. A=One visit every 30 to 45 days B=One visit every 60 to 90 days=One visit every 100 to 120 days

To help plan, use this formula to determine how much time to set aside for networking each month.

TOTAL TIME = Average Number of Visits per Month X 1.5 Hours

The time for each visit, 1.5 hours, includes planning time, driving time, waiting time, and meeting time. This is an average. The more experience gained in making referral visits, the less time they will take.

Networking with Family Members

Families can be a great source of leads because they interact with people their own age on a regular basis. If they are happy with the service their loved one receives, they will share that information with others. The profile of an average family member is typically a female who is 45-65 years old.

As a result of the information sharing among friends, it is possible to gain qualified leads. Friends help friends to work through the emotional difficulties of putting mom in a home. They think through the transition from a residential home into an assisted living facility, nursing home or continuing care retirement community. They talk frankly about the pros and cons of long-term care options, including the financial burden. If the care in your facility is good, the grapevine will definitely work in your favor. The friends network is a great benefit to you. A lot of education and information sharing takes place before the potential resident ever calls you.

The most common reason for a resident to leave a long-term care facility is hospitalization. As resident's age in place, their frailty increases. As a result, the need for acute medical care may arise. There may be times when a frail resident needs to be hospitalized. When a resident becomes hospitalized, the facility runs the risk of losing the resident. When a resident is hospitalized, the family will often decide their parent needs the increased care that may not be offered by the assisted living facility. They might be getting direction from a hospital discharge planner. If the discharge planner does not fully understand the capabilities of every facility, they may recommend a nursing home upon discharge. It is important that both families and discharge planners become aware of what services you can offer.

Hospitalized residents may not return to your facility for a variety of reasons. Some facilities forget about residents in the hospital. They don't visit hospitalized residents. They don't communicate to the family that the facility can continue to care for the resident. Others never consider alternatives to hospitalization once a resident requires certain levels of medical care. Sometimes, the family feels emotionally deserted by the facility. They never consider returning their parent to the facility. It is important that someone from the facility communicate with the family of a hospitalized resident. If the facility does so, it may very likely become a part of the decision-making process regarding what will happen to the resident when their hospital stay is over.

Networking with hospitalized residents and their families will enhance the facilities influence by communicating care and concern for a resident who considers your long-term care facility their home. Families will share this message with their friends and communicate with the hospital, the resident's doctor, and a wide variety of health-care professionals that your facility cares.

By being present and involved, the facility will be aware of the options the family is considering. As a result, it will likely be part of the decision making process.

Family networking is very effective in promoting customer satisfaction. When the facility finds ways to network with families, it promotes satisfaction by providing opportunities for families to resolve issues with the administrator, increasing rapport between family members and staff, and building trust between the family members and the community. In larger communities, the social worker may work with the marketing staff to make the hospital and family contacts. If there is no social worker, the marketing staff or the administrator should make these contacts.

There are two common reasons for dissatisfaction in a long-term care community. The first is poor communication and the second is unresolved issues. These can revolve around any number of things, but the two most common are resident care and dining services. When someone is dissatisfied, they most often talk to their friends first. Unhappy family members do not want someone they know to make the same mistake they did. It is said that a dissatisfied customer is likely to share their negative experience with at least *nine* other people.

Advertising

Advertising is a paid form of non-personal communication about an organization, good, service, or idea by an identified sponsor. It is used to reach the masses and fees are paid for space or time. The advantage of advertising is that it does reach a large number of potential clients but it has high, absolute costs and doesn't lend itself for giving good feedback. It informs by giving facts about the community and what services are provided. It persuades others to explore further or purchase the community's services. It reminds all who see the ad that the community is operating, offering services and spells out the location of the community.

Advertising can be very helpful in getting information out to large numbers of people, but to be effective, there must be strategy for it's use. Begin by determining your target audience and say in the ad what would be appealing to that target audience.

Once you decide whom to target, design the ad to get their attention. Once it gets attention, be sure it provides the information you want it to convey.

Pictures should pull people in and perk their interest. In the end, the ad should get the reader to do something, i.e. call the facility.

Marketing: Strategies for Inquiry Generation

1. Develop a sound strategy based on individual situations' objectives.

If the facility is brand new and/or under 50% occupied, the strategy should be fairly aggressive. If it is located in a populated area you may want to concentrate your energies on 80+ seniors and/or their adult children within certain perimeters by creating a direct mailing campaign.

Make sure to include a time line for your strategy and consider the possibility of multi-component campaign spread out over a pre-determined period of time. You may want to consider seasons and anticipated behaviors and mindsets related to each season.

2. The "List" is half the battle

Lists are only as strong as the criteria through which they are generated. Be sure to tell the people from whom you buy the list who you hope to reach. To what age ranges do you what to send information? What income ranges do you what to reach? Do you want a particular ad to go to the children of the potential resident? Do you want another to go directly to the potential resident?

3.Creative is the second half of the battle

The artwork must get noticed in order for the brochure to get opened. In order to get noticed, it must appeal to the targeted audience and create perceived value. The artwork can communicate visually what the text is also saying. If you are saying that your staff is compassionate toward old people, then the pictures should show an example of that, not the front of the building.

Personalization generates a sense of involvement and responsibility. Be sure your message is unique.

A. Local Radio

Advantages:
Relatively low cost
Targets specific audiences
Quick placement
Uses sound and intimacy effectively

Disadvantages:
No visual excitement
Exposure time is short

Message is "perishable"
Difficulty in conveying complex message to prospect
Competes for prospect's attention i.e. driving, working, relaxing
Best Placement:
Drive time
Run of Station

B. TV

Advantages:
Reach
Utilizes picture print
Target ability

Disadvantages:
High cost
Short exposure
Message short lived
Complex information hard to convey

Cable TV

Advantages:
Narrowcast
Viewers more responsive to direct marketing
More upscale market: spend 60% more on goods and services than normal
Cable can be a better buy than radio or print in terms of cost

Disadvantages:
Short exposure
Message short lived
Complex information hard to convey

C. Print
Newspaper
Advantages:
Excellent reach potential
Immediate prospect response

Coverage of local markets
Can be quickly changed
Relatively low cost

Disadvantages:
Competing for attention with other ads and articles
Cannot control placement on page
Short life span
Cannot target specific audience

Advertisements
Make the ad "work hard for you"
Involve the reader
Use headlines that entice the reader to the ad
Make a definite request and have a vehicle for response (i.e. coupon) if action is a goal
Avoid giving too much information (goal is for inquiry to want more)
Use response enhancers: 800 numbers & websites

Best Placement:
The Sunday paper, especially the food section or the TV Guide section are best.

Publications:
Select most effective/ appropriate publications. Major dailies, local publications (church bulletins, theater and/ or sports programs, weekly and free newspapers)

Take advantage of Special Sections and Editions. Placement strategies help get the most bang for the buck
Frequency—timing is everything. Use weekend and holidays.
Require tear sheets to be sent with invoicing

Community Publications:
Church bulletins, community bulletin boards, libraries, grocery stores, programs, theater, trailers and sporting events.
2. Advertorials
Effectively use this tool in the absence of Public Relations

Yellow Pages
Check your inquiries to see if this should be a part of the mix
Ad reps work on commission—don't let that influence what's best for you

D. Collateral & Promotional Tools
   1. Print
Image is everything and it's your printed collateral that delivers your image to potential customers.

Choose paper, design, type, and graphics that make a positive statement.

Reader-friendly fee schedules, maps, floor plans, amenities, contracts, forms, and resident agreements continue to deliver a message. Make the material consistent and identifiable. Be sure it is large enough for the elderly to read.

Chapter Seventeen

Marketing Plan

The marketing plan is similar to the management plan in that it requires thoughtful preparation and once completed, provides a road map for marketing strategies for the coming year. It is essential that a marketing plan be developed to provide information about the area around the community and to give direction for using your time and resources effectively. The following is an outline of what should be included in a comprehensive marketing plan.

Facility Description:
This section provides a brief overview of the facility; it's history, ownership, mission, and goals.

Situation Analysis: (SWOT)
Most often a situation analysis includes an honest review of the strengths, weaknesses, opportunities and threats faced by the business. The strengths are capabilities; resources and skills within the facility that will help you meet your goals. The facility weakness is just the opposite, anything about the facility that will prevent you from meeting your goals. Opportunities are perceived ways to meet the goals, to make additional sales or to capture more of the market share. Threats are things like competition, the economy or a new home health agency that would prevent you from meeting your goals.

Competitive review:
Gives information about the neighboring facilities, what they offer, their prices and how the facility compares.
Determination of Target Market:
It is important to determine who will qualify as a resident in the facility. This section should identify the minimum age and income for the potential

residents. It should also address the kind of treatment the facility can and will provide. The target market could also identify a radius from the facility where marketing efforts will be undertaken. Most assisted living facilities attract people from a five to ten mile radius of itself. Continuing care retirement communities have a larger primary market area.

Inventory Analysis:

Knowing what is renting and what is not is important. It is also good to know what is renting in neighboring long-term care facility as well. Perhaps the small rooms or the semi private rooms are harder to turn over than the larger private rooms. A strategy for renting these particular rooms would be important. You may want to reduce the price or offer an incentive for people to move in.

Market Analysis:

Normally this component is done by a company that looks at the target area, compares prices, room sizes, makes calls to age and income qualified potential residents or sends out questioners to the same. They are able to use census information along with survey results and their review of the competition to determine what the market wants. Everything will be reviewed including room sizes; location, price, amenities, activities and how many people would be willing to potentially move into your facility.

Consumer Research:

This is research that can be purchased or you can do it yourself around the topics of what a potential resident wants, how much they will be willing to pay for it and what expectations they have of the services they will receive for their money. There are also survey results available through a variety of companies and agencies.

Strategies for Lead Generation:

Advertising

Determine what kind of advertising will be done, when it will be done and how much it will cost. Include website, newspaper, collateral material and any sponsorship of events planned for the coming year.

Public Relations

Determine what events you will hold or participate in that will generate good public relations. Also project the costs for these events.

Direct Mail

Decide when you will send out a direct mailing to potential residents. Lists can be purchased of people who are age and income qualified who also live in the facility target area. If a marketing firm is used to create the piece

to send in the direct mailing, remember to estimate the cost for creations and publication as well as the postage required to send the mailing.
Networking
Set out a plan that will determine who will be seen, how they will be seen and how often they will be seen. Refer to the networking comments listed in the previous chapter to get a feel for how this can be accomplished.
Internal Marketing
Decide how often events will occur in house that are designed to be internal marketing efforts. Put together resident referral plans, family referral plans and staff referral plans that help generate sales. Include costs for these events.

Strategies for Sales:
Goals and Objectives
It is important to know how many rooms you expect will turn over in the course of a year. Using past history or industry benchmarks, decide how many residents will move out or die during the year leaving a room to rent/sale. Set goals for the replacement of those people that will enable the facility to remain 95% full at all times.
Marketing Staff
In this category list the number of staff members that will be involved in marketing and the functions they will provide.
Sales Office
Indicate where the office is and where a closing room might be.

Strategies for Marketing Management:
Systems and Procedures
Refer to policies that have been prepared and approved, the normal procedures for admission and how marketing will relate to the other departments to successfully bring new residents to the facility.
Lead Tracking Mechanisms
Describe how the lead tracking system works and how it can be an asset to keeping in touch with potential new residents.
Developing a marketing plan gives direction for the future while looking closely at the strengths and weaknesses of past performances. This plan and the management plan will serve as the cornerstone of the budget.

Chapter Eighteen

Nursing

Nursing is the most important department in the long-term care facility. It has more employees than any other department and provides a much needed service. More regulations are written regarding nursing and nursing care than any of the other disciplines.

Assessment

After marketing has persuaded a person to become a new resident of your facility, someone from the nursing department will perform an assessment of the person's needs. This assessment will serve as the starting point for the care the new resident will receive. The assessment tools may vary, but nearly all ask questions that provide a picture of three general areas: 1. Psychosocial and cognitive status. 2. Physical abilities. 3. Sensory impairments. Under the Psychosocial heading, questions are asked to try to determine a level of awareness, any traumatic events that may have occurred in the person's past, their emotional strength, their decision-making ability, and any wandering behavior they may display. Questions about the physical abilities deal with their ability to ambulate, their stability and history of falls, their ability to bath, groom, dress, toilet and feed themselves, their dietary needs, their physical endurance, their activity desires, their medication needs, housekeeping/ laundry needs and personal habits. Sensory impairment questions deal with vision, hearing and speech. After all the questions are answered, a score is tallied and from that score the nurse could tell if the resident is able to live independently, or is in need of assisted living services or is someone in need of a nursing home to meet their needs. Other assessment tools like the global deterioration scale and the mini mental exam assist the nurse in determining the needs of the potential resident.

Nursing homes are required to provide a more in depth assessment of their residents than assisted living facilities. They are required to make a comprehensive assessment of a resident's needs, using the Resident

Assessment Instrument (RAI) specified by the state in which they are licensed. The assessment should include at least the following:

(i) Identification and demographic information.

(ii) Customary routine.

(iii) Cognitive patterns.

(iv) Communication.

(v) Vision.

(vi) Mood and behavior patterns.

(vii) Psychosocial well-being.

(viii) Physical functioning and structural problems.

(ix) Continence.

(x) Disease diagnoses and health conditions.

(xi) Dental and nutritional status.

(xii) Skin condition.

(xiii) Activity pursuit.

(xiv) Medications.

(xv) Special treatments and procedures.

(xvi) Discharge potential.

(xvii) Documentation of summary information regarding the additional assessment performed through the resident assessment protocols.

(xviii) Documentation of participation in assessment.

The assessment process must include direct observation and communication with the resident, as well as communication with licensed and non-licensed direct care staff members on all shifts. Residents who have dementia may behave differently in the evening or at night than during the day. It is important to get feedback from all three shifts.

A nursing home may be required to conduct a comprehensive assessment of a resident in accordance with specific time frames. This is an example according to the Nursing Homes Regulations found in the Code of Federal Regulations section 483.20.

Within 14 calendar days after admission, excluding re-admissions in which there is no significant change in the resident's physical or mental condition. (For purposes of this section, re-admission means a return to the facility following a temporary absence for hospitalization or for therapeutic leave.)

(ii) Within 14 calendar days after the facility determines, or should have determined, that there has been a significant change in the resident's physical or mental condition. (For purposes of this section, a significant change means a major decline or improvement in the resident's status that will not normally resolve itself without further intervention by staff or by implementing standard disease-related clinical interventions, that has an impact on more than one area of the resident's health status, and requires interdisciplinary review or revision of the care plan, or both.)

(iii) Not less often than once every 12 months.

(c) Quarterly review assessment. A facility must assess a resident using the quarterly review instrument specified by the State and approved by CMS not less frequently than once every 3 months.

(d) Use. A facility must maintain all resident assessments completed within the previous 15 months in the resident's active record and use the results of the assessments to develop, review, and revise the resident's comprehensive plan f care.

(e) Coordination. A facility must coordinate assessments with the preadmission screening and resident review program under Medicaid in part 483, subpart C to the maximum extent practicable to avoid duplicative testing and effort.

(f) Automated data processing requirement.

(1) Encoding data. Within 7 days after a facility completes a resident's assessment, a facility must encode the following information for each resident in the facility:

(i) Admission assessment.

(ii) Annual assessment updates.

(iii) Significant change in status assessments.

(iv) Quarterly review assessments.

(v) A subset of items upon a resident's transfer, reentry, discharge, and death.

(vi) Background (face-sheet) information, if there is no admission assessment.[28]

Physician History and Physical

One important piece of information provided to the person making the assessment is a History and Physical Report completed by a physician. This is a sample History and Physical that would be appropriate for an assisted living facility. Note that the questions regarding conditions of care distinguish what a typical assisted living facility can handle as opposed to a nursing home that provides a higher level of care.

REPORT OF RESIDENT PHYSICAL EXAMINATION
NAME:
DATE OF PHYSICAL EXAMINATION:
ADDRESS:
TELEPHONE:
Height:_____Weight:_____BP:_____
Significant Medical History:
General physical condition:
Allergies (food, medicine, or other):
Is this person:
_____Ambulatory (physically and mentally capable of self-preservation by evacuating in response to an emergency without the assistance of another person, even if such resident may require the assistance of a wheelchair, walker, cane, prosthetic device, or a single verbal command to evacuate).
_____Nonambulatory (by reason of physical or mental impairment is not capable of self-preservation without the assistance of another person).
Does this individual have any of the following conditions or care needs?
Condition/Care Need   Yes No
Ventilator dependency.
Dermal ulcers III and IV.
If stage III is ulcer healing?
Intravenous therapy or injections directly into the vein.
If intermittent therapy please note and indicate expected time period.
Airborne infectious disease in a communicable state that requires isolation or special precautions to prevent transmission.
Psychotropic medications without appropriate diagnosis and treatment plans.
Nasogastric tubes
Gastric tubes
If yes, is person capable of independently feeding himself and caring for the tube?
Presents imminent physical threat or danger to self or others
Requires continuous licensed nursing care

Diagnosis or significant problems:
Recommendations for care:
Medications:
Diet:
Therapy:

Signature:_____Date:_____
    (Please print or type physician's name here)

Address (Street, City, State, Zip Code)
_____Tele-
phone:_____

ATTACHMENT I
REPORT OF TUBERCULOSIS SCREENING EVALUATION
    Name_____Birth date ____/____/_____
    Address_____
    Date and result of most recent Mantoux tuberculin skin test:
    Date:___/___/____mm of in duration_____
    2. Check here if previously positive and above information unknown_____
    3. Check here if exhibiting TB-like symptoms_____
    4. If TB skin test is 10 mm or greater (5mm in the HIV infected), previously positive or if TB-like symptoms exist, *respond to the following:*
    a. Date of last chest x-ray evaluation: Date:____/____/_____
    b. Is chest x-ray suggestive of active TB? *(circle one)* YES NO
    c. Were sputum smears collected and analyzed for the presence of Acid Fast Bacilli (AFB)? *(circle one)* YES NO
    d. If 4c is YES, were three consecutive smears negative for AFB? (circle one) YES NO
    5. Based on the above information, is this individual free of communicable TB? (circle one) YES NO
    6. Name of licensed physician, physician's designee or local health department official completing the evaluation:

    Print name_____number_____

7. Signature of license physician, physician's designee or local health department official completing evaluation:
Date:

The assessments, along with a history and physical report from physician help the nursing staff to determine what they need to do to meet the needs of the new resident. Where deficiencies are noted in abilities, a plan of care is written indicating how the facility will meet the needs of the resident. For instance, if a person were blind, the plan of care would indicate what the facility would do to assist them with ambulation, meals, activities etc. If they were someone who fell often, the plan of care would indicate what the facility would do to try to prevent these falls. This plan of care serves as a guide to the nursing staff to treat the resident in a particular fashion and indicates how the facility will meet the physical, mental, emotional and psychosocial needs of the residents and provide protection, guidance and supervision that will in turn promote a sense of security, promote involvement and meet the objectives of the service plan.

The physician's history and physical should indicate what medication the person is taking. If the resident wants the facility to be responsible for medication management, a physician's order is required that tells a nurse what to do. Forms called Medication Administration Records (MAR's) are used to indicate what medication is to be given at what dosage and how often. The form provides a space for the nurse to put her initials indicating that a medication had been given.

Finally, a quarterly review of the progress of the resident should be held to determine if they are having their needs met, if they are improving and if they are in the appropriate level of care. This is normally called a care conference or a family care plan meeting and it is normally open to the residents and family along with appropriate staff members. These staff members are often physicians, rehab therapists, the activity director, a social worker, the dietician, and others as appropriate. Any changes in the plan of care should be noted after this meeting and appropriate staff should be notified of the change.

Individualized Service Plan

In Virginia, in the assisted living facilities, the Individual Service Plan is completed upon admission and updated after each quarterly meeting or when there is a change in the condition of the resident. The following is an example of the form the state provides for this function.

VDSS MODEL FORM—ALF

INDIVIDUALIZED SERVICE PLAN

If applicable: Medicaid#_____DMAS Provider ID#_____

Resident's Name:_____

Name of ALF:_____

See reverse side for signatures and additional information.

Description of needs is based upon the UAI, medical reports, and any additional assessments necessary to meet the care needs of the resident.

A.If the resident lives in a building housing 19 or fewer residents, does the resident need to have a staff member awake and on duty at night? Yes No

Description of Needs and Date Identified:

Services to be provided:

Persons who will Provide Services:

When and Where Services will be Provided:

Expected Outcomes/Goals (Include Time Frames):

Description of Needs and Date Identified:

SIGNATURES:

_____/_____

Staff Person Who Completed Plan Date Plan Completed Resident/Date

Licensed Health Care Professional (630.J) Date Other, if any, Involved in Development of Plan Date_____

(For Assisted Living Care Residents) (Specify Title/Relationship)

PLAN REVIEW/MODIFICATIONS

NOTE: Changes in plan should be initialed by staff person making change, resident, and for assisted living care residents, licensed health care professional

Staff Person Designated to Review, Monitor, Ensure Implementation, and Make Appropriate Modifications to Plan:_____

Dates Implementation Monitored and Initials:_____/

_____

SIGNATURES:

_____

Staff Person Who Completed Plan Review Date Staff Person Who Completed Plan Review Date_____

Comprehensive Care Plan

In nursing homes, the Comprehensive Care Plan replaces this Individualized Service Plan form. After reviewing the physician admission orders, that spell out diet, medications and care required, the nurse doing the initial assessment uses a Minimum Data Set (MDS) form or a uniform data set that is used to assess the resident's ability to function in all of the activities of daily living. The Comprehensive Care Plan must include measurable objectives and set timetables to meet the resident's medical, nursing and psychosocial needs identified in the assessments and the physician admission orders.

This meeting is usually the responsibility of the MDS coordinator, who is an RN, and is required at least quarterly for each resident, but may be called sooner if there is a change in the condition of the resident that requires a change in the goals established in the previous Care Plan. Each discipline is required to comment on the goals set and how they plan to achieve them within their particular scope of practice.

Medication Administration Plan

It is best to develop a Medication Administration Plan that can serve as a formal plan or policy for the facility. This plan, if followed, will give guidance to the nursing personnel. Examples of topics that might be in the plan are:

Standard Operating Procedures for Medication Management
Contacting Physicians related to written or verbal orders
Physicians Order Sheets (POS)

Methods to Verify Accurate Order transcription to Medication
Administration Records (MARs)
Review of Physicians Order Sheets by Licensed Nurse

Prevention of Use of Discontinued, Outdated, Damaged, or Contaminated
Medications
End of Month Pharmacy Delivery, Verification of Delivery and
Procedures for Returning Medications

Methods to Maintain Adequate Medication Supply
Pharmacy labeling, filling, and delivery
On Call Pharmacy Services

Methods to Monitor Medication Administration and Effective Use
of MARs for Documentation
Pharmacy Consultant Reviews
Licensed Nurse Review Monthly
Documentation after each Medication Pass

Plan for Proper Disposal of Medication
Pharmacy Agreement
Other Means of Medication Disposal

Responsibility for Reporting Adverse Reactions, Suspected Side Effects,
And Effectiveness of Medications to Primary Physician
Licensed Nurses
Pharmacy Role

Administration of Medication and Related Services
New Admission/Re-Admission Orders
Primary Physician Notification
Contents of Physician Orders
Charting Verbal/Oral Orders
Medication Storage, location, refrigeration
Administration of Medication and Related Services
UAI Resident Qualification
Pharmacy Container Use
Pre-pouring
Administering Medications per Physician Instructions
Medication Storage Containers
Sample Medication Packaging
Over-the-Counter Medication Storage
Annual Training for Medication Aides

Documentation of Medication Administration Record (MAR) and
Treatment Administration Record (TAR)

By following this plan, along with normally accepted nursing practices,
the nursing care provided in either a nursing facility or an assisted living
facility should be adequate. It is essential that an LPN be on staff to provide
medication. It is preferable that an RN be on staff to serve as the director of

nursing. Regulations for nursing homes require that an RN be present at least eight hours per day. Some states allow med-tech's to administer certain medications in assisted living facilities. This is an area of great concern. It is essential that the medications that the staff provides be stored in a container that can lock in an area free from dampness or abnormal temperatures. Most pharmacies provide a med cart that will serve this purpose. When passing the medications, even at night, the area should be light enough to read container labels. The person who takes the medication out of the pharmacy container must give it to the resident within two hours. It should not be removed from the container by one person and delivered by another. It is essential that the staff pass medications according to a physician's order. There should be a doctor's order form that he signs. It makes clear what is to be given in what dosage and when. The pharmacy that takes that order should then indicate the same on the label of the medication container.

The following paragraphs highlight the most essential parts of the plan. However, by reviewing the appropriate regulations and establishing policies, each long-term care facility can develop their own complete medication management plan.

When a new resident is admitted or there is a re-admission to the facility, the Licensed Nurse should contact the resident's doctor to verify the admitting orders before any medications are given. Once the orders have been verified, a Physician Order Sheet (POS) should be faxed to the pharmacy for them to fill the new prescription. The pharmacy then will deliver the medications to be administered.

It is the responsibility of the licensed nurse to communicate with the resident's doctor regarding the effectiveness of prescribed medications, any suspected adverse reactions or side effects of such medications. When new medications are given, the nurses must be observant for adverse side effects.

The consultant pharmacist will communicate with the resident's doctor any concerns they may have regarding a particular medication the physician has prescribed. The following information may appear in this regard: all medications the resident is taking, examination of dosage, strength, route, frequency, duration and time of day medications are taken, consideration of potential interactions of drugs or food/drink, consideration of potential negative effects of drugs resulting from a resident's medical condition(s), consideration of whether PRN medications are still needed, consideration of whether additional monitoring or testing may be helpful, consideration of potential adverse effects of the medications, identification of that which may be questionable such as a) similar medications being taken, b) different medications being used to treat the same condition, c) what seems an excessive number of medications (poly-pharmacy), and d) what seems an exceptionally high drug dosage.

Any action taken by the doctor after being contacted by the pharmacist should be recorded and kept in the resident's record.

All physician orders for the administration of prescription and over-the-counter medications, dietary supplements, and treatments or other procedures, whether verbal or written, should contain specific information. This includes the name of the resident, the date of the order, the name of the drug, route, dosage, strength, frequency of administration, and should also include the diagnosis, condition, or indications for which the medication was prescribed.

Any time the doctor gives a verbal order, this order should be noted (charted) by a nurse.

A nurse should review the POS monthly, completed prior to midnight on the last day of each month. This review is conducted by the LN and serves to help ensure the five rights for every resident: right resident, right drug, right dose, right route, and right time. In addition, the LN is responsible for checking that physician's have signed the original of any telephone order within 10 days of the order. The following steps should be included in each POS monthly review to help insure there have been no medication changes overlooked:

1. Check that each order is still current and has not been discontinued.
2. Check the beginning and stop dates of each order.
3. Compare the POS with any orders that have been written since the POS was printed, and add new orders to it.
4. Compare the POS to the MAR and TAR with changes as appropriate.
5. Compare the previous month's MAR and TAR to the current MAR, TAR, and POS with changes as appropriate.
6. Mark on the MAR and TAR any times or block off any dates that must be flagged for each shift for the entire month.
7. Sign with full signature and title, as well as, date the bottom of each page of the MAR and TAR indicating that it was reviewed.
8. Verify that medication orders have been accurately transcribed to the MAR.

Along with the monthly review of medications by the nurse, there should be a semi-annual review of all medication by the consulting pharmacist. They normally review all of the prescription and over-the-counter medications, supplements, and treatments. They may observe and/or interview the resident as a part of the review if appropriate. The review includes the following areas:

a. All medications the resident is taking and could be taking, both routine and PRN.

b. Examination of dosage, strength, route, frequency, duration, and times of medication use.

c. Documentation of actual and potential interactions of drugs with each other or drugs with foods or drink.

d. Documentation of actual or potential adverse effects of drugs from resident's medical condition other than the one being treated.

e. Consideration of whether PRN medications are still needed or clarification related to their use.

f. Consideration of whether the resident needs further monitoring or testing.

g. Documentation of actual or potential adverse or unwanted side effects.

h. Identification of questionable areas such as

    1. similar medications being taken

    2. different medications used to treat the same condition

    3. poly-pharmacy

    4. high or low drug dosages

When administering medication, the following documentation should be provided:

Name of resident, date prescribed, drug name, dosage, strength, route and how often the medication is to be given. When the mediation is given, the person giving it must indicate the date, time and their initials. If medication is discontinued or changed, or medication errors occur, or there are significant effects of an error, these should be noted. The names and initials of all staff that administer medications should also be noted. In the event of an adverse drug reaction or medication error, first aid should be administered according to instruction of a physician, pharmacist or the poison control center. The resident's physician must be notified as soon as possible.

The following is a form from the state of Virginia that serves as a Medication Administration Record.

VDSS MODEL FORM—ALF
    MEDICATION ADMINISTRATION RECORD PAGE_____OF_____
    NAME OF RESIDENT_____
    Month/Year:
INSTRUCTIONS: Use one block for each medication. In MEDICATION column, include drug product name, strength of drug, date prescribed, dosage, route, how often medication is to be taken, any special instructions, and name of prescribing physician.

The staff person administering the medication must initial the appropriate block to show the date and time the medication was given. In the ADDITIONAL INFORMATION space at the bottom of the sheet, note if a medication is discontinued or changed, any medication errors or omissions (include reason), any significant adverse effects, and the date(s) of these occurrences. The staff person making the note should initial it. On the back of the form; list the names and initials of all staff administering medication to the resident.

Medication	Time	1	2	3	4	5	6	7	8	9	10	11	12	13	14	15	16	17	18	19	20	21	22	23	24			

ADDITIONAL INFORMATION:
Name & Initials:
Name & Initials:
Name & Initials:
Name & Initials:
Name & Initials:
    The form should have 31 days on it. Each medication to be given is listed on the left and the nurse would initial in the appropriate space when she/he

has given the medication. The names and initials are often found on the back of the form. The purpose here is to be able to see who gave the medication.

Medications, diets, medical procedures, and treatments should not be started, changed or discontinued without an order from the physician. Often, the physician will send a verbal or oral order to the facility changing a medication. Once that is done, the facility should send the physician a form for their signature so that a written record of this change is retained in the resident medical chart. Occasionally, these orders are for an "as needed" medication called a "PRN" medication. In this case the physician spells out the conditions under which the medication can be given on the form and the nurses follow those orders. These orders need to be signed by the physician within 10 days. The following is an example of this Oral order from that is acceptable for assisted living facilities in the state of Virginia.

VDSS MODEL FORM—ALF
DOCUMENTATION OF PHYSICIAN'S ORAL ORDER
FOR PRN (*AS NEEDED*) MEDICATION
NAME OF RESIDENT:
PHYSICIAN GIVING ORDER:
DATE OF ORDER:
NAME AND STRENGTH OF MEDICATION:
PHYSICIAN'S INSTRUCTIONS:
1. SYMPTOMS THAT MIGHT INDICATE USE OF THE MEDICATION:
2. MEDICATION DOSAGE:
3. TIME FRAMES THE MEDICATION IS TO BE GIVEN IN A 24-HOUR PERIOD:
4. DIRECTIONS IF SYMPTOMS PERSIST:
5. ANY ADDITIONAL INSTRUCTIONS:
NAME OF FACILITY STAFF RECEIVING ORDER:
PRINT:
SIGNATURE:
032-05-530/1 (Revised ½)

Staffing for Assisted Living Facilities
We have talked about staffing issues earlier, but it is good to touch on it as it applies to nursing at this time. A common complaint, no matter how many staff members are assigned to work with the residents, is that there is not enough staff. People simply assume that this will be the case and jump

quickly to that conclusion when an injury occurs. Generally, the rule of thumb for assisted living facilities is that one nurse aide will meet the needs of ten residents. In some facilities, med techs are used to do both the care and passing of medication. Licensed practical nurses are used to pass medications, give treatments and supervise nurse aides. Having a registered nurse on staff to serve as the director of nursing in an assisted living facility is truly an advantage. In most cases, it is not required in assisted living facilities. Having a registered nurse on staff provides the facility with a department director with more education and better assessment and administrative skills than LPN's normally possess. This can be valuable in numerous ways.

It is good to cross train staff to be able to use them productively. Let me provide an example of how this worked in facilities I managed. The nurse aides who assisted residents with bathing, dressing, grooming, ambulation and toileting were trained as med-techs. That means they also passed some of the routine medications. In addition, they served meals and cleaned up afterwards. The also did laundry and assisted in activities. On every shift they also did rounds, collected trash, tidied up in the resident rooms and vacuumed the dining and lobby areas. By virtue of their involvement in nearly all aspects of the lives of their residents, they were very helpful when it came to make changes to care plans. They knew how often the residents were bathed, what medication they took, side effects of the medication, how much they ate and what activities they enjoyed.

Staffing for Nursing Facilities

OBRA is a law that dictates standards of care for nursing. These standards help determine what the nursing staff will be required to do for all residents. Some of the required positions for nursing facilities are listed below. In some cases, these may not be full time positions, and often times they are contracted positions:

The administrator is a full time position regardless of the size of the facility. The duties and responsibilities of the administrator are to be the one person responsible for all that happens in the facility.

The medical director can be less than full time and may be contracted. Their duties include acting as an advisor to the administrator or director of nursing, acting as a liaison with other physicians, providing the services of a physician for new residents as necessary and serving on the Medical Quality Assurance Committee. They are also called upon to approve policies that deal with resident care.

The director of nursing is a full time position. He/she is a registered nurse who is irresponsible for the supervision of the nursing department. Some of the duties include reviewing the facility statements regarding the types of care the facility will provide, developing policies, ensuring that the resident's nursing needs are met, participating in interdisciplinary team assessments and care plans, and reviewing the nursing requirements for new residents.

Registered Nurse. There must be a registered nurse on duty at least eight hours per day seven days per week.

The MDS Coordinator can be part time position or one that is combined with other responsibilities based on the size of the facility. His/her responsibility is to complete the MDS assessment and to develop a care plan for each resident. Each discipline has a section of its own, but the coordinator is responsible for seeing that it all completed within the appropriate time frame.

The quality assurance coordinator can be apart time position or one combined with others.

The staff educator is usually provided by an RN and can be a part time position. They provide ongoing training required for the nursing staff and also offer in-service training to other department employees around issues like infection control.

The social worker is full time if the facility is over 120 beds. The job of the social worker is to assist the residents in attaining their highest physical, mental and psychosocial well-being. In order to make that possible, the social worker must be involved in an initial assessment of the potential resident's needs. After an interview, they must develop a social history that is included in the resident chart. The social worker should be a part of the interdisciplinary team that does care planning so that they can identify the needs of the resident from their perspective. They are often the point of contact the families have with the facility regarding when care plan meetings will occur. They also keep families informed of any problems or potential problems they may be aware of with the resident. If they notice any changes in affect, behavior or personality, the social worker will interact with nursing and make a note of her observation in the resident chart. The social worker is also the staff member who assists residents and families by being aware of community services that might be of use to them. In this role, they are often directly involved with residents, families and even staff members as a counselor.

The medical records clerk to file closed records and to thin open files. This can be a part time position, but it must be someone with organizational skills and knowledge of nursing terms and practice.

The pharmacist can be a contract employee or company who is responsible for filling prescriptions, delivering the medication to the facility and reviewing the drug regimen for each resident monthly. Once the pharmacist fills the physician order, they dispense the medication into a card, or dose package and label it with appropriate information such as the patient name, the name of the medication, the strength of the medication, the name of the physician who prescribed the medication, the quantity of the medication dispensed along with it's date of expiration. This medication is then brought to the facility and placed in an appropriate storage container for safety and distribution by the nursing staff. Finally, the pharmacist who is contracted to review charts and med passes, should also serve on the quality assurance team.

The dietician can be part time or contracted. They serve as a professional who can provide consultations for the physicians on residents who exhibit significant weight changes. Their primary purpose is review the diets used in the facility and to recommend any special diets for residents.

Direct care staff are nurse aides who assist residents with activities of daily living. They assist with bathing, dressing, grooming, toileting, ambulation, eating and communicating. They are the employees that provide the hands on care to meet the most basic needs of the residents.

Discharge of Residents

Assisted living facilities have a limit to what nursing services they can provide. Each state sets these limits. Most often, if someone has a stage three or four dermal ulcer, they must seek care at a nursing home. If they require intravenous therapy or injections into the vein, they must receive these services in a nursing home. Residents who have an air borne infectious disease in a communicable state that requires isolation or special precautions by the nurse to prevent the spread of the disease should go to a nursing facility where their needs can be met. Feeding tubes like nasogastric tubes or gastric tubes require special skills and training. People who require these feeding devices should go to a nursing home. Some assisted living facilities are able to keep residents who are non-ambulatory, but that is dependent on the building type and the local fire marshal. If someone presents an imminent threat to themselves or others, they should be sent to a facility where they can get appropriate psychiatric attention. People who require continuous licensed nursing care need to be in a nursing home. These are some examples but each state that offers a license to an assisted living facility should also have a list of who is an appropriate resident based on the facility and the kind of service it provides. Nursing homes are the appropriate setting for people who no longer have their needs met in an assisted living facility.

If a resident's health gets to the point where they can no longer stay at the facility, discharge procedures need to begin to assist them in finding a facility where their needs can be met. The following is an example from the state of Virginia.

VDSS MODEL FORM—ALF

DISCHARGED

RESIDENTSNAME:_____

1. Date of discharge notification to resident: _____ notification:_____

2. Date of discharge notification to personal representative, if any:_____

Name of personal representative:

Notification:

3. Reason(s) for the discharge:

4. Actions taken by the facility to assist the resident in the discharge and relocation process:

5. Date of the discharge:

(Destination name and address):

6. If emergency discharge, name(s) of person(s) notified, other than specified above, and date(s) of notification:

Signed by: _____ Date:_____

(Licensee or administrator)

(Name of Facility)_____

NOTE: The original of this statement is to be given to the resident or his personal representative. A copy is to be retained in the resident's record.

032-05-527/1 (Revised ½)

Nursing Facilities may also have limitations to the services they provide. Some facilities do not provide skilled nursing care. Most do not have ventilator units or special TB units. In these cases, if the needs of the resident cannot be met by the facility, it must assist the family in finding a more appropriate setting.

Part Four
General Information

Chapter Nineteen

Resident Rights:

The OBRA regulations of 1987 indicate that all residents of long-term care facilities have certain rights and responsibilities. These rights are to a dignified existence, self-determination, and communication with and access to persons and services inside and outside the facility. How these rights are exercised is also spelled out in a variety of federal and state laws and regulations. Exercising rights, according to Windborn Davis, means that residents have autonomy and choice, to the extent possible, over how they wish to live their everyday lives and receive care.[29] It is easy to imagine that what a resident may want and what an institution may be able to provide could come into conflict at some point. Facilities are institutions that have numerous regulations dictating how care must be provided on one hand and residents who want to remain as independent as possible on the other. Finding the balance may be an ethical, moral or even a legal question depending upon the situation.

A quick review of Section 483.10 of the Code of Federal Regulations indicates in what manner the residents are to be treated and what power they possess over decision-making. To insure that potential and current residents understand these rights, the long-term care facilities are required to display the list of Resident Rights and Responsibilities and to review them with all potential residents orally and in writing. For a person who has dementia, the review should also be with the person who has been designated as the Power of Attorney or Guardian. For those who are deaf, the facility must let them read each item. For those who are blind, the rights must be read to them. For those who do not speak English, an interpreter must be provided so that they do understand these essential rights. Any time a facility reviews these rights with a resident, the resident should acknowledge the review in writing.

The first right of any resident is the right to exercise his or her rights as a resident of the facility and as a citizen or resident of the United States.

Residents also have the *right to be free from interference, coercion, discrimination, or reprisal from the facility in exercising their rights.* In the case of a resident adjudged incompetent under the laws of a state by a court of competent jurisdiction, the rights of the resident are exercised by the person appointed under State law to act on the resident's behalf. If a resident who has not been adjudged incompetent by the State court, any legal-surrogate designated in accordance with State law may exercise the resident's rights to the extent provided by State law.

It is the responsibility of the administrator to make sure that all staff members understand this. If a resident does not want to comply with a policy or regulation, there are appropriate procedures within the regulations for documentation of behavior, assessments, counseling, care plan conferences and discharge planning to assist the resident to find a more suitable living situation, without resorting to restrictions, isolation or reduction of privileges. The problem seems to arise when employees of long-term care facilities take on the role of the parent, telling the resident what to do when and how, and then dulling our punishment when the response is not appropriate.

The right to inspect records. The resident or his or her legal representative has the right by asking for or in writing, to access all records pertaining to himself or herself including current clinical records within 24 hours, excluding weekends and holidays. If they would like a copy of these records, the facility would make them available to them at a fee not to exceed what the community standard photocopies of the records might be within two working days advance notice. The resident has the right to inspect and purchase copies of all their records.

This right is also listed in the Health Insurance Portability and Accountability Act of 1996 where it indicates that everyone has the right to have access to their records, and to make copies or to have them made.

The resident has the right to be *fully informed in language that he or she can understand of his or her total health status, including but not limited to, his or her medical condition.*

The resident has the right to refuse treatment, to refuse to participate in experimental research, and to formulate an advance directive.

If the facility is a participant in the Medicaid program, it must inform each resident who is entitled to Medicaid benefits, in writing, at the time of admission to the nursing facility or, when the resident becomes eligible for Medicaid of the items and services that are included in the facility services under the state plan and for which the resident may not be charged; those other items and services that the facility offers and for which the resident may be charged, and the amount of charges for those services; and inform each resident when changes are made to the appropriate regulations regarding this area.

If the facility is a Medicare provider, it must inform each resident before, or at the time of admission, and periodically during the resident's stay, of services available in the facility and of charges for those services, including any charges for services not covered under Medicare or by the facility's per diem rate.

These requirements help residents and families understand what is being paid for and what responsibilities belong to the facility as opposed to the resident or families.

The facility must furnish a written description of *legal rights* which includes a description of the manner of protecting personal funds, a description of the requirements and procedures for establishing eligibility for Medicaid, including the right to request an assessment under section 1924(c) which determines the extent of a couple's non-exempt resources at the time of institutionalization and attributes to the community spouse an equitable share of resources which cannot be considered available for payment toward the cost of the institutionalized spouse's medical care in his or her process of spending down to Medicaid eligibility levels, and a posting of names, addresses, and telephone numbers of all pertinent state client advocacy groups such as the State survey and certification agency, the State licensure office, the State ombudsman program, the protection and advocacy network, and the Medicaid fraud control unit; and a statement that the resident may file a complaint with the state survey and certification agency concerning resident abuse, neglect, misappropriation of resident property in the facility, and non-compliance with the advance directives requirements.

The facility must have written policies and procedures regarding advance directives that inform and provide written information to all adult residents concerning the right to accept or refuse medical or surgical treatment and, at the individual's option, to formulate an advance directive. The facility should also have policies to implement advance directives and applicable State law. Facilities are permitted to contract with other entities to furnish this information but are still legally responsible for ensuring that the requirements of this section are met. If an adult individual is incapacitated at the time of admission and is unable to receive information (due to the incapacitating condition or a mental disorder) or articulate whether or not he or she has executed an advance directive, the facility may give advance directive information to the individual's family or surrogate in the same manner that it issues other materials about policies and procedures to the family of the incapacitated individual or to a surrogate or other concerned persons in accordance with State law. The facility is obligated to provide this information to the individual once he or she is no longer incapacitated or unable to receive such information. It is always important to know what the resident wants for him or herself rather than depend upon someone else for their opinion.

The facility must inform each resident of the name, specialty, and way of contacting the physician responsible for his or her care.

The facility must prominently display in the facility written information, and provide to residents and applicants for admission oral and written information about how to apply for and use Medicare and Medicaid benefits, and how to receive refunds for previous payments covered by such benefits.
Notification of changes.

The facility must immediately inform the resident; consult with the resident's physician; and if known, notify the resident's legal representative or an interested family member when there is an accident involving the resident which results in injury and has the potential for requiring physician intervention; a significant change in the resident's physical, mental, or psychosocial status; a need to alter treatment significantly; or a decision to transfer or discharge the resident from the facility.

The facility must also promptly notify the resident and, if known, the resident's legal representative or interested family member when there is a change in room or roommate assignment or a change in resident rights under Federal or State law or regulations.

The facility must record and periodically update the address and phone number of the resident's legal representative or interested family member. Keeping this information current assists the facility in making contact when necessary.

If the long-term care facility has a distinct section, admission to that composite distinct part must be disclosed in its admission agreement, its physical configuration, including the various locations that comprise the composite distinct part, and it must specify the policies that apply to room changes between its different locations.
Protection of resident funds:

The resident has *the right to manage his or her financial affairs*, and the facility may not require residents to deposit their personal funds with the facility.

Upon written authorization of a resident, the facility must, however, hold, safeguard, manage, and account for the personal funds of the resident deposited with the facility.

The facility must deposit any residents' personal funds in excess of $50 in an interest bearing account (or accounts) that is separate from any of the facility's operating accounts, and that credits all interest earned on resident's funds to that account. (In pooled accounts, there must be a separate accounting for each resident's share.) If the funds are less than $50, the facility is not required to keep the funds in an interest-bearing account. However, the facility must establish and maintain a system that assures a full and complete and separate accounting, according to generally accepted accounting principles, of each resident's personal funds entrusted to the facility on the resident's behalf. This system must preclude any commingling of resident funds with facility funds or with the funds of any person other than another resident. The individual financial record must be available through quarterly statements and on request to the resident or his or her legal representative. In addition, the facility must notify each resident that receives Medicaid benefits when the amount in the resident's account reaches $200 less than the SSI resource limit for one person; and that, if the amount in the account, in addition to the value of the resident's other nonexempt resources, reaches the SSI resource limit for one person, the resident may lose eligibility for Medicaid or SSI.

Upon the death of a resident with a personal fund deposited with the facility, the facility must convey within 30 days the resident's funds, and a final accounting of those funds, to the individual or probate jurisdiction administering the resident's estate.

The facility must purchase a surety bond, or otherwise provide assurance satisfactory to the secretary, to assure the security of all personal funds of residents deposited with the facility.

The facility may not impose a charge against the personal funds of a resident for any item or service for which payment is made under Medicaid or Medicare (except for applicable deductible and coinsurance amounts.) The facility may charge the resident for requested services that are more expensive than or in excess of covered services in accordance with Sec. 489.32 of this chapter of the Code of Federal Regulations.

During the course of a covered Medicare or Medicaid stay, facilities may not charge a resident for the following categories of items and services:

(A) Nursing services as required at Sec. 483.30 of this subpart.

(B) Dietary services as required at Sec. 483.35 of this subpart.

(C) An activities program as required at Sec. 483.15(f) of this subpart.

(D) Room/bed maintenance services.

(E) Routine personal hygiene items and services as required to meet the needs of residents, including, but not limited to, hair hygiene supplies, comb, brush, bath soap, disinfecting soaps or specialized cleansing agents when indicated to treat special skin problems or to fight infection, razor, shaving cream, toothbrush, toothpaste, denture adhesive, denture cleaner, dental floss, moisturizing lotion, tissues, cotton balls, cotton swabs, deodorant, incontinence care and supplies, sanitary napkins and related supplies, towels, washcloths, hospital gowns, over the counter drugs, hair and nail hygiene services, bathing, and basic personal laundry.

(F) Medically-related social services as required at Sec. 483.15(g) of this subpart.

Listed below are general categories and examples of items and services that the facility may charge to residents' funds if they are requested by a resident, if the facility informs the resident that there will be a charge, and if payment is not made by Medicare or Medicaid:

(A) Telephone.

(B) Television/radio for personal use.

(C) Personal comfort items, including smoking materials, notions and novelties, and confections.

(D) Cosmetic and grooming items and services in excess of those for which payment is made under Medicaid or Medicare.

(E) Personal clothing.

(F) Personal reading matter.

(G) Gifts purchased on behalf of a resident.

(H) Flowers and plants.

(I) Social events and entertainment offered outside the scope of the activities program, provided under Sec. 483.15(f) of this subpart.

(J) Noncovered special care services such as privately hired nurses or aides.

(K) Private room, except when therapeutically required (for example, isolation for infection control).

(L) Specially prepared or alternative food requested instead of the food generally prepared by the facility, as required by Sec. 483.35 of this subpart.

The facility must not charge a resident (or his or her representative) for any item or service not requested by the resident.

The facility must not require a resident (or his or her representative) to request any item or service as a condition of admission or continued stay.

The facility must inform the resident (or his or her representative) requesting an item or service for which a charge will be made that there will be a charge for the item or service and what the charge will be.

Free choice
The resident has the *right to:*

1. *choose a personal attending physician*
2. *be fully informed in advance about care and treatment and of any changes in that care or treatment that may affect the resident's well-being*

and unless adjudged incompetent or otherwise found to be incapacitated under the laws of the State, 3. *participate in planning care and treatment or changes in care and treatment.*

Privacy and confidentiality
The resident has *the right to personal privacy and confidentiality of his or her personal and clinical records.*

Personal privacy includes accommodations, medical treatment, written and telephone communications, personal care, visits, and meetings of family and resident groups, but this does not require the facility to provide a private room for each resident. The resident may approve or refuse the release of personal and clinical records to any individual outside the facility. This refusal to the release of personal and clinical records does not apply when the resident is transferred to another health care institution; or the record release is required by law.

Once again, The HIPAA regulations also address this issue. One of the primary functions of the act is to protect private health information. This is addressed in a variety of ways in long-term care facilities, but residents have the ability to restrict who has access to their protected health information and can request that certain people not be informed of their condition. The privacy of the resident's condition is central to this act as it should be when long-term care facilities create policies around quality of life and quality of care.

Grievances
A resident has the *right to voice grievances without discrimination or reprisal.* Such grievances include those with respect to treatment, which has been furnished as well as that which has not been furnished; and prompt

efforts by the facility to resolve grievances the resident may have, including those with respect to the behavior of other residents. It is important to develop a grievance policy to share with residents upon admission so that they know who to see and what to expect from the reporting of a problem.

Examination of survey results

A resident has the *right to examine the results of the most recent survey of the facility* conducted by Federal or State surveyors and any plan of correction in effect with respect to the facility. The facility must make the results available for examination in a place readily accessible to residents. It should also post a notice of their availability; and indicate where a resident might receive information from agencies acting as their advocates, and be afforded the opportunity to contact these agencies.

Work

The resident has *the right to refuse to perform services for the facility.* They can perform services for the facility, if he or she chooses, when the facility has documented the need or desire for work in the plan of care. If the plan does document the desire to work, it should then specify the nature of the services performed and whether the services are voluntary or paid. If the services are paid, the compensation for those services should be at or above prevailing rates, and the and the resident should indicate that he/she agrees to the work arrangement described in the plan of care.

Mail

The resident has *the right to privacy in written communications*, including the right to send and promptly receive mail that is unopened; and have access to stationery, postage, and writing implements at the resident's own expense.

Access and visitation rights

The resident has *the right and the facility must provide immediate access to* any resident by the following:

(i) Any representative of the Secretary;

(ii) Any representative of the State:

(iii) The resident's individual physician;

(iv) The State long-term care ombudsman (established under section 307(a)(12) of the Older Americans Act of 1965);

(v) The agency responsible for the protection and advocacy system for developmentally disabled individuals (established under part C of the Developmental Disabilities Assistance and Bill of Rights Act);

(vi) The agency responsible for the protection and advocacy system for mentally ill individuals (established under the Protection and Advocacy for Mentally Ill Individuals Act);

(vii) Subject to the resident's right to deny or withdraw consent at any time, immediate family or other relatives of the resident; and

(viii) Subject to reasonable restrictions and the resident's right to deny or withdraw consent at any time, others who are visiting with the consent of the resident.

(2) The facility must provide reasonable access to any resident by any entity or individual that provides health, social, legal, or other services to the resident, subject to the resident's right to deny or withdraw consent at any time.

The facility must allow representatives of the State Ombudsman, described in paragraph (j)(1)(iv) of this section, to examine a resident's clinical records with the permission of the resident or the resident's legal representative, and consistent with State law.

Telephone.

The resident *has the right to have reasonable access to the use of a telephone* where calls can be made without being overheard.

Personal property.

The resident has the *right to retain and use personal possessions*, including some furnishings, and appropriate clothing, as space permits, unless to do so would infringe upon the rights or health and safety of other residents.

Married couples.

The resident has the *right to share a room with his or her spouse* when married residents live in the same facility and both spouses consent to the arrangement.

Self-Administration of Drugs.

An individual resident *may self-administer drugs* if the interdisciplinary team has determined that this practice is safe.

Refusal of certain transfers.

(1) An individual has the right to refuse a transfer to another room within the facility, if the purpose of the transfer is to relocate:

(i) A resident of a SNF from the distinct part of the institution that is a SNF to a part of the institution that is not a SNF, or

(ii) A resident of a NF from the distinct part of the institution that is a NF to a distinct part of the institution that is a SNF.

The right to establish a resident council that determines its' duties and may include:

Developing a grievance procedure.

Communicating concerns of other residents to administration.
Obtaining information for the administrator.
Sharing information with the administrator
Identifying problems
Assisting in solutions
Acting as a liaison with the community.[30]

Many of the policies that determine how long-term care facilities operate are based upon these aforementioned lists of rights and responsibilities. Likewise, many of the regulations governing the industry are also based upon an interpretation of these rights. The wise administrator is one who reads them and understands them and how they impact the life of the facility.

Chapter Twenty

Agencies, Associations and Helpful Organizations

The following is a list of some agencies or organizations that will be of help to a administrator as you seek to better understand the needs of the elderly and what is already available in most communities to meet those needs.

"Area Agencies of Ageing" are government-funded agencies throughout the United States. They provide a variety of services such as transportation, case management, a meal program, senior centers, protective services, information and referral and an ombudsman program.

Some of these agencies are called "senior services" of a particular area. Many times these services are provided at a reduced rate due to the government funding.

Adult day health care centers provide day care, socialization, supervision, food, structured activities, and medication distribution to the older adults who spend all of or a portion of the day in these centers. I mentioned that the last church I served had such a center. I would encourage you to investigate within your state what requirements there are for providing a similar service to your community.

Associations are organizations that provide information and raise funds around a particular area of interest. Examples include the American Diabetes Association, the American Dental Association, the American Heart Association, the American Lung Association and the Alzheimer's Association.

American Association of Retired Persons is a well-known association that provides many services including insurance, pharmacy, financial, travel and information. It's greatest influence on behalf of the elderly is political. Through the many chapters the association has throughout the country, it is able to quickly rally support by phone, letter and e-mail for one particular bill or another at every level of government. It also offers support for the elderly and of course, financial discounts in many businesses.

Case managers are a new profession of people who help families and individuals identify, coordinate and monitor the community services a person needs as they age. They are aware of government services and regulations.

Durable medical equipment is sold by many different companies. This equipment is essentially assistive devices that help a person remain independent, such as walkers, shower chairs, wheel chairs, canes and motorized carts.

Elder Law Attorneys practice a particular kind of law that enables them to assist the elderly with will preparation, guardianship, power of attorney, living wills, help with taxes, assistance with Medicaid and Medicare benefits and estate planning.

Home Health Care provides skilled nursing care and rehabilatative or therapeutic services, including speech, occupational and physical therapy in a person's home or in an assisted living facility. Also included can be companion, personal care, and homemaker services. These services provide non-medical assistance to persons whose physical condition prevents their performance of routine personal tasks. Services many include assistance with bathing, dressing, light housekeeping, meal preparation and grocery shopping.

Lions Club is a service organization devoted to helping bring sight to the blind and hearing to the deaf. It raises money to provide free testing of sight and hearing and to provide glasses and hearing aides at a reduced rate.

Ombudsman Programs are designed to assist our older adults who live in assisted living or nursing facilities. They investigate complaints by the older adult or those made on their behalf.

Personal Electronic Response Systems are electronic monitoring systems that allow a person to press a button worn around their neck in case they are unable to reach the phone in an emergency.

Protective Services are usually a part of an Area Agency on Aging. They exist to investigate cases of suspected abuse, exploitation, abandonment or neglect. They work in concert with other agencies to correct problems they find.

Respite care is in home assistance allowing time off for family care givers providing full time care. This service can be provided by a home health agency. Many assisted living facilities also offer this short-term stay of less than 30 days. Some associations offer financial assistance to families who are caring for their loved one that would enable them to pay for a home health aid to come into the home to allow them to get away for banking, shopping or just to relax.

Senior Assessment is a program that is often hospital based where an assessment is made of the physical and mental conditions of an older person. By virtue of this assessment, appropriate services, medication or placement can be suggested.

Senior Centers are centers that offer a variety of services including socialization, meals and educational programs.

Support groups are groups that have regularly scheduled meetings that provide members an opportunity to discuss their difficulties and learn coping or adaptive techniques. I have mentioned already how important and appropriate grief support can be in the setting of the church facility. It is also appropriate to open these facilities to other organizations that are seeking space such as the Alzheimer's Association or Heart Association.

The Alzheimer's and Related Disorders Association provides support, and services such as material, support groups, financial aide for adult day care and in home care. The purpose of this organization is two fold: 1. To raise money for research. 2. To provide support to victims and families.

The American Heart Association provides similar services as those mentioned above. It too is designed to raise money for research and provide assistance to victims.

American Lung Association is similar to those already mentioned. Each has a particular area of interest and a mission to change the dreadful effects of a particular disease.

The Diabetes Association is much like those above. These agencies are all listed in the telephone book under services or associations.

It is to your advantage to gather together as much recourse information as possible so as to be better prepared to meet the needs of the congregation. Most cities have Mayor's Commission on Ageing or other such commissions that can be of great assistance to you. Call for information and volunteer to sit on the commission!

Chapter Twenty-One

Medical Terms

It is important for the long-term care administrator to understanding medical terminology. The following is a list of medically related prefixes, suffixes, words and abbreviations that are common in this industry.

Prefixes:

AD	toward or at
Angio	to a vessel
Ante	before
Anti	against
Apo	away from
Auto	by oneself or same
Bi	two or twice
Bio	related to life
Brady	to slow
Cardi	pertaining to the heart
Cervico	pertaining to the neck
Chiro	pertaining to the hand
Chole	pertaining to bile
Cranio	pertaining to the head
Cysto	pertaining to the bladder
Derm	pertaining to the skin
Endo	within or inner
Entero	pertaining to the intestines
Gastro	pertaining to the stomach
Glyco	relation to sweetness
Hemi	half
Hemo	blood
Hyper	excessive, above normal
Hypo	below normal

Inter	between
Intra	within
Labio	pertaining to the lip
Mono	one
Myel	pertaining to the spinal cord
Myo	pertaining to the muscle
Naso	pertaining to the nose or nasal passages
Nephro	pertaining to the kidney
Neuro	pertaining to the nerves
Opto	relating to vision
Osteo	pertaining to bone
Oto	pertaining to hearing, ear
Para	two parts, beyond and beside
Patho	disease
Pneumo	pertaining to the lungs
Procto	pertaining to the rectum
Quadra	four
Rhino	nose
Semi	partial
Thoracic	pertaining to the chest or thorax
Uro	pertaining to urine

Suffixes:

-algia	pain
-cyte	cell
-ectomy	removal of organ or gland
-emesis	vomiting
-ism	abnormal condition
-itis	infection of or inflammation
-osis	diseased condition
-otomy	incision, or cut
-phobia	fear or dread that is unreasonable
-rrhage	excessive discharge
-plasty	surgical repair
-trophy	development or nourishment
-uria	urine

Common terms:

Activities of Daily Living are bathing, grooming, eating, dressing, walking, toileting and communicating.

Acute is an intense, painful, serious condition.

Ambulatory is able to ambulate, walk about.

Amputation is the removal of a limb.

Aseptic is free from disease.

Atrophy is the wasting away of tissue or an organ or limb.

Benign is not recurrent.

Blood Pressure is the pressure of the blood on the walls of the blood vessels.

Chemotherapy is the treatment of a disease with chemical compounds.

Chronic is prolonged.

Colostomy is when a portion of the colon is opened through the skin to divert the flow of feces.

Comatose is like being in a coma.

Communicable is capable of spreading from one person to another.

Contagious is communicable by contact.

Contusion is a bruise.

Decubitus ulcer is a bedsore or pressure ulcer.

Dehydrated is when the body tissues lose too much water.

Diagnosis is a medical decision reached regarding a condition after an examination.

Edema is when the tissues retain too much water.

Hematoma is a swelling that contains blood.

Hemmorrhage is the discharge of blood from blood vessels.

Incontinent is the lack of proper bowl or bladder control.

Jaundice is the yellowness of the skin and whites of the eyes due to bile pigment in the blood.

Laceration is a skin tear.

Malignant is resisting treatment and threatening to produce ill health or death.

Metastasis is the spread of cells or bacteria to other organs.

Obese is when one is at least 20% beyond a normal weight.

Prognosis is the probability of an outcome.

Prone is lying horizontal with face and palms of hands down.

Supine is lying on the back with face and palms up.

Toxic is poisonous.

Vital Signs are body temperature, blood pressure, pulse and respiration.

Glossary

Accrual basis accounting is an adjustment process used to record revenue and expense in the period in which they are earned or incurred.

The administrator is the one person responsible for all that happens in the facility.

Advance directives are written instructions concerning the right to accept or refuse medical or surgical treatment. They give nursing and medical personnel instructions regarding treatment in the event the resident is unable to communicate these desires.

The Age Discrimination Act of 1978 says that applicants over 40 and under 70 are also protected from discrimination.

Alzheimer's Disease, the largest cause of dementia, is a progressive brain disorder affecting memory, thought, behavior, personality and eventually, muscle control.
Aphasia is the inability to interpret and understand words.

Arthritis is an inflammation of a joint

Assessments are done by nursing personnel as a part of the admission process and at other times as needed. The assessment tools may vary, but nearly all ask questions that provide a picture of three general areas: 1. Psychosocial and cognitive status. 2. Physical abilities. 3. Sensory impairments.

Cancer is most often referred to as a malignant tumor: Skin cancer is the most prevalent cancer in both men and women, followed by prostate cancer in men and breast cancer in women. Lung cancer, however, causes the most deaths in both men and women.

Cardiovascular Disease has two major types. The first is artery disease and the second is vein disease. The most significant cause of artery disease is the thickening and hardening of the artery walls by deposits of fatty materials. The second type, vein disease, involves the formation of blood clots.

Cash basis accounting is the form used to balance a personal checkbook. It's also the form of accounting used to pay individual income tax. Revenues or deposits are recognized in the checkbook when one actually receives cash or deposits cash in the bank account. Expenses are recognized when cash is paid, such as when a check is written or cash is withdrawn.

Cerebrovascular accidents (CVA's), are more commonly known as a stroke.

The Civil Rights Act prohibits employers from discriminating against potential employees based on race, color, religion, sex, or national origin.

Clinical depression is a whole body disorder. It can affect the way you think as well as the way you feel, both physically and mentally.

Continuous Quality Improvement is a data driven process for improving performance.

Controlling, as an administrative function, is fixing problems once they are identified. It is coming up with the answer and making the changes necessary to keep the community moving in the right direction.

Dementia is a term that broadly defines cognitive loss.

A dietitian is someone who is qualified based upon either registration by the Commission on Dietetic Registration of the American Dietetic Association, or on the basis of education, training, or experience in identification of dietary needs, planning, and implementation of dietary programs.

Direct Care Staff are nurse aides who assist residents with activities of daily living.

Directing is oversight. As an administrative function, it is taking care of the day-to-day problems that arise.

The director of nursing is a full time position. He/she is a registered nurse who is irresponsible for the supervision of the nursing department. Some of the duties include reviewing the facility statements regarding the types of care the facility will provide, developing policies, ensuring that the resident's nursing needs are met, participating in interdisciplinary team assessments and care plans, and reviewing the nursing requirements for new residents.

Dysphasia is the inability to speak.

Endogenous depression is depression which occurs without a precipitating event.

Evaluating as an administrative function includes not only how employees are performing, but also how the whole community is functioning. This includes finances, staff moral, resident census and satisfaction.

Forecasting is predicting what might happen that could impact on the facility.

GAAP is an acronym for Generally Accepted Accounting Principles.
The General Ledger normally includes these three statements: The *Income Statement* that tells the administrator whether the revenues were enough to cover the expenses. The typical accounting understanding of income is not simply the money that comes into the facility, but revenues minus expense. The second statement is the *Balance Sheet*. This statement is a summary of the assets, liabilities and capital accounts. The standard formula for this is that assets are equal to liabilities plus capital. Assets are the things the facility owns that can be sold or turned into cash somehow within twelve months. Liabilities are those bills that must be paid within the next twelve months. This includes utilities, food, nursing supplies, anything that must be paid within a year. Capital includes money invested in the facility by the owner along with any net income that has been put back into the facility. The third statement is the *Statement of Change* that indicates the transactions that occurred over the past month. It would show how the amount of working capital has changed over the month and why.
HCFA is an acronym for The Health Care Finance Administration.
HHS is an acronym for Health Care Financing Administration

Inquiries is a marketing term for people who inquire about your community or your services.

A job description should include a job title that defines the position, job summary that briefly defines responsibilities and working relationships, any educational requirements or certifications required, a list of significant duties and responsibilities and a place for the new employee to sign and date.

The management plan will provide the road map for the future of the facility. It is an instrument that is developed with support of the Board. It begins with the mission statement and then sets plans in place to meet that mission.

Material Safety Data Sheets (MSDS) are sheets of paper that chemical manufactures send with their chemicals giving important safety information about their product. They are to be placed in a book that is easily located in an emergency.

The marketing plan is similar to the management plan in that it requires thoughtful preparation and once completed, provides a road map for marketing strategies for the coming year.

The medical director can be less than full time and may be contracted. Their duties include acting as an advisor to the administrator or director of nursing, acting as a liaison with other physicians, providing the services of a physician for new residents as necessary and serving on the Medical Quality Assurance Committee. They are also called upon to approve policies that deal with resident care.

Medication Administration Records (MAR's) are used to indicate what medication is to be given at what dosage and how often. The form provides a space for the nurse to put her initials indicating that a medication had been given.
Networking is a strategy used for building ongoing, mutually beneficial relationships.

Organizing is deciding how much staff is necessary to meets the needs of the residents in a long-term care community and how they will relate to one another.

Orthostatic hypotension is being light headed when you rise from bed or chair too quickly.

The Occupational Safety and Health Act (OSHA) of 1970 was an act that was designed to protect the employee from injury. It has established standards for safety in the work place. OSHA has the right to inspect the facility at any time for compliance with its regulations and the records of injuries to the employees. This record is to be kept on a form called a Log and Summary of Occupational Injuries and Illnesses. Those injuries recorded on this log are injuries resulting in loss of work, disability or death.

Par level is a basic needs level for stocking items such as food or medical supplies. By establishing a particular level needed at all times, one can order to bring the facility back up to that level.

Physician Order Sheet (POS) is a form on which the nurse writes out a physician's verbal order. It is sent to the doctor's office via. fax for signature before it is placed on the resident's chart.

Planning is an essential function of administration. It enables the business to work toward a goal, to make decisions based on where it wants to go in the future and how it will get there.

Presbycusis is a term used to describe any hearing impairment, especially as it relates to high frequency tones.

Presbyopia is a loss in accommodation that decreases the ability for the eye to focus on close-up objects. The pupil diameter becomes smaller, causing less light to enter the eye.

Referral source is someone who can refer to your community. Typically this would be a physician or discharge planner.

Resident rights: The OBRA regulations of 1987 indicate that all residents of long-term care facilities have certain rights and responsibilities. These rights are to a dignified existence, self-determination, and communication with and access to persons and services inside and outside the facility. Staffing is the process of recruiting, interviewing, hiring and scheduling employees.

Treatment Administration Record (TAR) is a record kept by the nurse indicating what treatment was given and when.

Bibliography

Allen, James. *Nursing Home Administration*. New York, 1992.

Anderson, Kenneth and Herbert Anderson. *All our Losses, All our Griefs*. Philadelphia, 1983.

Bossidy, Larry and Charan, Ram. *Execution the Discipline of Getting Things Done*. New York, 2002.

Code of Federal Regulations.

Collins, Jim. *Good to Great*. New York. 2001.

Davis, Winborn. *The Introduction to Health Care Administration*. Bossier City. 2000.

Finkelstein, Sydney. *Why Smart Executives Fail and What We Can Learn From Their Mistakes*. New York, 2003.

Kane,R.L., Ouslander, J. G. and Abrass, I.B. *Essentials of Clinical Geriatrics* 2nd ed. New York, 1989.

Katz, D. & Kahn, R. L. *The Social Psychology of Organizations*. New York, 1967.

Koenig, Harold. *Aging and God*. New York, 1994.

Leaf, Alexander. "Getting Old," Scientific America 1973.

Sterling DA, O'Conner JA, Bonadies J. "Geriatric Falls: injury severity is high and disproportionate to mechanism." *Journal of Trauma-Injury Infection and Critical Care* 2001; 50:116-119.

US Census Bureau.

Printed in the United States
209615BV00001B/340/A